BURGUNDY TRAVEL GUIDE
2024

Burgundy Unveiled: Your Ultimate Travel Companion To the Heart of France: Exploring the Rich Heritage, Hidden Gems, Culinary and Wine Odyssey

Mark E. Fears

ALL RIGHTS RESERVED.

No part of this publication may be reproduced, distributed or transmitted in any form or by any means including photocopying, recording or other electronic or mechanical methods without the prior written permission of the publisher, except in the case of brief quotations embedded in critical reviews and certain other noncommercial uses permitted by copyright law.

Copyright © Mark E. Fears, 2023

Table Of Contents

My Memorable Vacation To Burgundy

1. Introduction

1.1 Greetings from Burgundy

1.3 A Synopsis of Burgundy's History

1.4. Cultural Importance

2. Important Preparation For Your Travel

2.1 The Ideal Season to Visit Burgundy

2.2. Length of Stay

2.3 Information on Travel Documents And Visas

2.4 Cost and Budgeting Considerations

2.5 Packing Essentials

3. Gastronomic Treats And Beverages

3.1 Examining Burgundy's Gastronomic Traditions

3.2 Customary Burgundian Food

    3.2.1 Desserts from Burgundy

    3.2.2 Burgundian cheeses

    3.2.3 Typical Ingredients from Burgundy

    3.3 Local Grocery Stores and Dining Out

3.4 Wine Types and Visits to Vineyards

3.5 Beer and Other Regional Drinks

4. Dining And Nightlife

4.1 Restaurants in Burgundy

4.2 Fine Dining Establishments and Establishments with Michelin stars

4.3 Rneighborhood Bistros and Classic Restaurants

4.4 Wine Shops and Wineries

4.5 Places for Entertainment and Nightlife

4.5.1 Nightclubs

4.5.2 Bars and Pubs

4.5.3 Live Music Locations

4.5.4 Additional Entertainment Locations

5. Shopping In Burgundy

5.1 Burgundy Retail Therapy

5.2 Local Artists' Workshops and Crafts

5.3 Vintage Shops and Antique Stores

5.4 Local Goods and Souvenirs

Regions of Burgundy

6. Côte-d'Or

6.1 **Dijon**

    6.1.1 "Castles and Palaces"

    6.1.2 Must Visit Historic Locations

    6.1.3 Museums and galleries of fine art

    6.1.4 Gardens and Parks:

    6.1.5 The Côte d'Or's natural landmarks include:

    6.1.6 Côte-d'Or Markets and Shopping:

6.2 Beaune

    6.2.1 "Beaune - History and Wine"

    6.2.2 Hospices of Beaune

    6.2.3 Auction of Beaune Wines

    6.2.4 Cellars and Wine Tasting Experiences in Beaune

    6.2.5 Historic Streets and Buildings

6.3. Wine and Charm at Nuits-Saint-Georges

    6.3.1 Wineries and wine cellars

    6.3.2 Historic sites and monuments

    6.3.3 Gastronomy and Local Cuisine in Nuits-Saint-Georges

    6.3.4 Nuits-Saint-Georges Local Festivals and Wine-Related Events

6.4 Additional Cities and Towns

7. Saône-et-Loire

7.1 Macon

    7.1.1 City Highlights

    7.1.2 Activities Outside

7.2 The Abbey and History of Cluny

    7.2.1 Cluny Abbey

    7.2.2 Medieval Buildings and Cultural Heritage

    7.2.3 Cluny Today

7.3 Autun

    7.3.1 Roman Architecture

    7.3.2 Natural Wonders

7.4 Additional Villages and Towns

8. Yonne

8.1. Auxerre

    8.1.1 "Historic Attractions"

    8.1.2 *Cultural Celebrations*

8.2 Vézelay - Spirituality and Pilgrimage

    8.2.1 Vezélay Abbey

    8.2.2 Baselique Sainte-Marie-Madeleine

    8.2.3 Routes of Pilgrimage and Spiritual Journeys

    8.2.4 Local customs and pilgrimage occasions

8.3 Chablis

    8.3.1 Vineyards and Wine Tasting

    8.3.2 Local Food

8.4 Additional Cities and Towns

9. Transportation And Costs

9.1 How to Travel to Burgundy

9.2 Buses and Trains for Public Transportation

9.3 Driving Advice and Car Rentals

9.4 Routes for Bicycling and Riding

9.5 Options for Ride-sharing and Taxi Services

9.6 Travel Expenses and Cheap Travel Advice

10. Accommodation And Prices

10.1 Accommodation Styles

10.2 Resorts and Hotels

10.3 Bed and (B&Bs)

10.4 Holiday Homes and Vacation Rentals

10.5 Outdoor lodging and Camping

10.6 Lodging Prices and Booking Advice

11. Outdoor Recreation

11.1 Discovering Burgundy's Natural Beauty

11.2 Trails for Hiking and Walking

11.3 Routes for Bikes and Cyclists

11.4 River and Water-related Activities

11.5 Wildlife Observation and Natural Areas

11.6 Aerial Adventures and Hot Air Balloon Rides

12. Events and Festivals

12.1 Grapes Harvest Festivals

12.2 Festivals of Music and Art

12.3 Wine Festival and Harvest Event

12.4 Historical Reenactments and customary celebrations

13. Perfect 7-14 Days Itinerary

13.1 Day by Day 7-Days Itinerary with Highlights

13.2 Recommendations that Are Off the Beaten Path

13.3 Ideas to Make the Most of Your Time

14. Practical Advice and Suggestions

14.1 Information on Health and Safety

14.2 Language and Regional Protocol

14.3 Currency and Financial Issues

14.4 Communication and the Internet

14.5 Highlights of Local Customs and Culture

My Memorable Vacation To Burgundy

My unforgettable trip to Burgundy was an unforgettable excursion through the heart of this alluring province. I was immersed in a world of history, culture, and natural beauty that forever changed the way I felt the moment I stepped foot in Burgundy.

My first impression of Burgundy's allure was its magnificent vineyards, which extended as far as the eye could reach. I had the chance to visit renowned wineries and sample some of the world's best Pinot Noir and Chardonnay wines while touring the Côte d'Or. Every sip was a revelation, a well-balanced mix of flavors and aromas that showcased the terroir and the steadfastness of generations of winemakers.

The picturesque towns and ancient cities of Burgundy were like entering a medieval fairy tale. One of the highlights was Beaune, with its cobblestone streets and vibrant rooftops. A marvel of Gothic and Renaissance architecture, the Hospices de Beaune served as a representation of the area's dedication to compassion and altruism. I took a leisurely stroll through the markets, enjoying the local cheeses and eating delicious foods like Coq au Vin.

Burgundy's natural splendor also mesmerized me. A wilderness of beautiful forests and clear lakes, the Morvan Regional Natural Park was one of the places I explored. The experience of hiking in this pristine environment was soul-nourishing, and I was in awe of the Morvan's calm beauty.

A leisurely boat ride on the Canal de Bourgogne was one of the highlights of my trip to Burgundy. I experienced a tremendous sense of tranquility and connectedness to nature as I floated along the bank lined with trees. It was a peaceful trip that nicely encapsulated the spirit of the area.

During my visit, I got to know friendly, hospitable locals who shared my enthusiasm for Burgundy. My experience was made richer by their tales and customs, which gave me the impression that I was more than simply a visitor but also a transient inhabitant of this amazing location.

My trip to Burgundy was a symphony of food, culture, and the natural world. It was a journey that gave me a deep appreciation for the region's rich cultural legacy and natural beauty in addition to allowing me to sample world-class wines and delectable cuisine. I'll treasure that memory for the rest of my life, and I can't wait to go back to Burgundy and experience its allure once more.

1. Introduction

1.1 Greetings from Burgundy

Welcome to Burgundy, a region known for its fine gastronomy, world-class wines, and rich history. Burgundy, or "Bourgogne" in French, is a region in the center of France that captures the mind and satisfies the senses. This charming region, whose history dates back to the Roman Empire, was instrumental in forming French culture and heritage.

Burgundy is well known for its beautiful scenery, quaint villages, and ancient cities. Some of the world's best wines are produced in the vines that dot the rolling hills. The renowned Côte d'Or, also known as the "Golden Slope," is where the area's elite vineyards are located. Fine Pinot Noir and Chardonnay wines are produced in this region thanks to the terroir, a singular synthesis of soil, climate, and tradition.

Burgundy's cuisine is a true gourmet treat. Coq au Vin and Boeuf Bourguignon are two rich, substantial dishes that are popular worldwide. Food experts adore the region's native cheeses, notably Epoisses and Cîteaux. Every meal offers the chance to enjoy Burgundy's delectable cuisine and world-class wines.

Burgundy's historical legacy is reflected in its architecture. Towns like Beaune and Dijon's medieval beauty transport travelers back in time. Beautiful cathedrals, like the one in Autun, highlight the area's cultural and religious past. Reflecting the area's dedication to philanthropy, the spectacular Hospices de Beaune is a masterpiece of Gothic and Renaissance architecture.

Burgundy is a region of natural beauty in addition to its historical and culinary delights. For hikers and outdoor lovers, the Morvan Regional Natural Park offers pure nature. The charming Canal de Bourgogne meanders through the area, offering relaxing bike rides along its tree-lined banks and gorgeous boat tours.

Welcome to Burgundy, a region rich in culture, cuisine, and natural beauty that weaves together a beguiling tapestry of experiences. This area welcomes visitors to learn about its history, savor its cuisine, and take in the enduring beauty of its landscapes.

1.2 Geography And Climate

Burgundy, in the center of France, is a region with an interesting and varied landscape and climate. This 31,500 square kilometer area of central France is divided among the Yonne, Côte-d'Or, Saône-et-Loire, and Nièvre departments. Its geological features are magnificent and extremely diverse.

Burgundy's topography features lush plains, tall forests, and undulating hills. The Morvan Massif, a hilly region in the northwest of the area clothed in lush flora, is one of the region's most recognizable geological features. The vineyard-covered slopes of the Côte d'Or to the east, which are renowned for producing some of the most sought-after wines in the world, stand in stark contrast to this harsh landscape.

The climate of Burgundy is essential to the creation of its world-famous wines. A temperate continental climate with distinct seasons prevails in the area. The warm summers enable grapes to ripen perfectly, while the occasionally chilly winters guarantee that the vines go into a necessary dormancy. The Pinot Noir and Chardonnay grapes that have made Burgundy's wines famous may be grown in this environment thanks to the region's diverse soils.

The Yonne and Saône rivers in particular are essential to the region's geographical makeup. They offer not just breathtaking scenery but also crucial rivers for agriculture and transportation. The center of Burgundy is traversed by the Canal de Bourgogne, which links the Saône and the Seine and provides lovely chances for leisurely boating.

A distinctive biodiversity has grown as a result of Burgundy's varied topography. With its extensive forests and clear lakes, the Morvan Regional Natural Park is a refuge for those who love the outdoors. In this protected natural area, visitors can explore hiking routes, see a variety of wildlife, and take in the serene serenity.

1.3 A Synopsis of Burgundy's History

Burgundy's history is a tapestry made of grandiosity, rivalry, and transition. Located in east-central France, this area has witnessed several crucial turning points in European history.

During the Roman era, when Burgundy was known as Gallia Lugdunensis, its origins can be found. With vibrant cities and a complex road system, it was a Roman province and a crucial piece of the Roman Empire. The region saw the slow rise of the Kingdom of the Burgundians following the fall of the Roman Empire, which eventually served as the foundation for the Duchy of Burgundy.

The development of the mighty House of Burgundy in the ninth and tenth centuries is the most important period in Burgundy's history. The Duchy of Burgundy expanded its power and wealth throughout the reigns of leaders like Richard the Justiciar and Robert I, becoming as a major force in medieval Europe. During this time, the renowned Burgundian Court, a hub of culture and refinement, was founded in Dijon.

Burgundy had a tremendous transformation in the 15th century. The Burgundian State reached its pinnacle as a result of Duke Philip the Good's marriage to Isabella of Portugal. As a result of the Burgundian Court's support for the arts, masterworks like Jan van Eyck and Rogier van der Weyden were produced. But after Charles the Bold died in 1477, the dynasty's influence started to wane, creating a complicated web of political intrigue and inheritance.

Later, European wars used Burgundy as a theater of operations, particularly the Franco-Spanish War and the Hundred Years' War. Burgundy's status as a sovereign state came to an end with the signing of the Treaty of Nijmegen in 1678, which eventually brought the area under French rule.

The cultural legacy and importance of Burgundy persisted after the loss of political independence. Its gastronomic customs, wines, and architectural wonders never stopped influencing not only France but the entire world. The Burgundian Dukes' extensive cultural sponsorship and rich heritage left a lasting impression on European aesthetics and art.

1.4. Cultural Importance

The cultural significance of Burgundy is a blend of historical treasures, gastronomic prowess, and creative accomplishments that have permanently influenced both French and world culture. Burgundy is a cultural treasure that never ceases to enthrall and inspire, from the gastronomic traditions of the area to its architectural wonders and artistic heritage.

Burgundian cuisine is one of the most renowned characteristics of the culture. Rich, savory cuisine is synonymous with the area. French food has grown to rely on dishes like Coq au Vin, a decadent chicken stew made with red wine, and Boeuf Bourguignon, a robust beef stew. The world-famous native cheeses of Burgundy, such as Epoisses and Cîteaux, are evidence of the region's outstanding culinary prowess. The region has a long-standing farm-to-table dining culture, where delectable, seasonally-inspired dishes are made with fresh ingredients.

The famed wines of Burgundy are also inextricably linked to the region's cultural significance. Some of the most coveted and renowned wines on the planet are produced by the region's vineyards. Outstanding Pinot Noir and Chardonnay wines are made possible by the terroir, a blend of land, climate, and tradition. Wine collectors and experts adore the wines produced by the Côte d'Or's vineyards, particularly those in Clos Vougeot and Romanée-Conti.

Burgundy is home to an incredible collection of old structures and monuments. The Hospices de Beaune, a magnificent example of Gothic and Renaissance architecture, is proof of the area's dedication to compassion and altruism. With their attractive alleys and well-preserved structures, the medieval cities of Beaune and Dijon transport visitors to a different era. Cathedrals in the area, like the one in Autun, serve as examples of Burgundy's artistic and religious heritage.

The rich cultural heritage of Burgundy is present in the field of art as well. During the 15th century, the Burgundian Court flourished as a hub of creative innovation thanks to the support of the wealthy Dukes. The Northern Renaissance was influenced by famous artists like Jan van Eyck and Rogier van der Weyden who produced masterpieces there.

2. Important Preparation For Your Travel

2.1 The Ideal Season to Visit Burgundy

In order to properly appreciate the beauty and pleasures of Burgundy, picking the optimum time to travel there is crucial. Burgundy is a year-round destination due to its climate and the nature of its attractions, but depending on your interests, some seasons provide specific advantages.

Burgundy is most beautiful in the spring, from March through May. The region is covered in a vivid green as the vines emerge from their winter hibernation. The grapevine's bud and the environment are decorated with vibrant wildflowers during this time of rebirth. Wine enthusiasts should visit now to see the grapes' development and budding. The Morvan Regional Natural Park is a great place to go bicycling and trekking because of the temperate temperatures.

The busiest travel season is in the summer (June to August), and for good reason. Warm and sunny conditions make it the perfect time of year to visit the historic villages of Burgundy, cruise the Canal de Bourgogne, and take part in outdoor events. Since it's the grape-growing season and the vineyards are lush, numerous wineries offer tours and tastings. However, because this is a busy travel season, it is crucial to reserve lodging and activities far in advance.

Wine lovers favor the fall (September through November) as the best time to drink wine. During this time, the grape harvest, or "vendange," occurs, and you can see the vines come to life with activity. Vineyards are turning vibrant colors of crimson and gold throughout the beautiful fall season. As the freshly harvested grapes are processed and the wineries are busy, this is the ideal time for wine sampling. Although it's still lovely outside, finding lodging is simpler than it is in the summer.

Burgundy's winter season, from December to February, is more sedate and private. The old villages of Burgundy nevertheless have appeal despite the barrenness of the vineyards. The cooler temperatures offer the chance to spend cosy evenings by the fireplace at historic inns and indulge in hearty, rich Burgundian fare. Winter can be a wonderful time to travel if you're looking for isolation and a deeper understanding of the culture and history of the area.

2.2. Length of Stay

The intensity of your research and the experiences you want will determine how long you remain in Burgundy. Burgundy has a variety of activities to accommodate different durations of stay, whether you have a few days or a few weeks.

For a Short stay (2–3 Days): For those wishing to experience the highlights of Burgundy, a brief stay is ideal. Visit the Hospices de Beaune, spend the day strolling through the quaint town of Beaune, and indulge in wine tastings at nearby wineries. Another day can be devoted to leisurely boat rides on the Canal de Bourgogne and lovely drives through vineyards. This little visit will offer you a lovely overview of the area.

For a Week-Long Trip (5-7 Days): You can explore more of Burgundy's beauties with a week on your hands. Visit additional vineyards and wineries, stroll through the Morvan Regional Natural Park, and explore the old city of Dijon. For a longer wine experience, plan day visits to nearby towns like Chablis and Chalon-sur-Saône. This time frame enables a thorough investigation of the area.

If you have more time, you can fully immerse yourself in the **Burgundian way of life on an extended visit (10–14 days).** Explore the lesser-known communities, more remote wineries, and the magnificent countryside in addition to the activities indicated above. Due to the length of your stay, you can take your time exploring the area's attractions, relaxing, and making new discoveries.

The length of your time in Burgundy ultimately depends on your interests and how much you want to learn about the people, places, and food of the area. Whether you opt for a quick weekend trip, a weeklong vacation, or a longer stay, Burgundy's attraction and charm are sure to leave you with priceless memories and a deep respect for this extraordinary place.

2.3 Information on Travel Documents And Visas

Burgundy, France travel papers and visa requirements should be carefully considered. France is a member of the Schengen Area, which makes it easier for some passport holders to travel throughout numerous European nations. Here is a thorough list of everything you require:

**1. Passport: **Confirm that your passport is valid for at least six months after the day you intend to leave France. If you are a citizen of the EU or a Schengen nation, entry may only require your ID card.

2. Visa: Visas are not required for stays of up to 90 days for tourists or business by citizens of the European Union (EU), European Economic Area (EEA), and a few other nations. You must, however, apply for a Schengen visa in advance through the French consulate or embassy in your country of residence if you are from a nation that needs one.

3. Residence Permit: You may need a long-stay visa or residence permit if you intend to stay in France for some time longer than 90 days or for a reason other than tourism or business (such as studying or working). The particular requirements will vary depending on why you are visiting.

4. Travel insurance: It is advisable to have complete travel insurance that includes trip cancellation and medical costs. For entry, several nations could demand proof of travel insurance.

5. Entry and Exit criteria: Be aware of any COVID-19-related rules as well as the most recent entry and exit criteria as they may change, particularly during a pandemic.

**6. Carry copies of your passport, visa, travel insurance, and any pertinent itineraries as additional documentation. Additionally, keeping digital copies safely saved is an excellent idea.

To ensure you have all the essential paperwork for a hassle-free trip to Burgundy, don't forget to check the most recent visa and travel requirements with the French embassy or consulate in your home country.

2.4 Cost and Budgeting Considerations

It's crucial to take into account your budget when organizing your vacation to Burgundy and to be aware of the costs involved in visiting this stunning part of France. Here is a list of the primary costs you'll incur:

1. Accommodations: There are many different types of lodging available in Burgundy, ranging in price from inexpensive hostels and guesthouses to opulent château hotels and winery estates. Depending on your preferences, you should budget €50 to €200 or more every night.

2. Dining: While it can be a lovely gastronomic experience, dining in Burgundy can be expensive. While Michelin-starred restaurants can be much more expensive, a three-course lunch at a mid-range restaurant may cost between €30 and €60 per person.

3. Transportation: Depending on how you decide to get around, your transportation prices may vary. The cost of a train ticket in France can range from €20 to €100 or more, depending on the distance and class. Renting a car gives you more flexibility, but keep in mind that you'll need money for parking, gas, and tolls.

**4. Wine tastings: In Burgundy, you must visit wineries and partake in tastings. Depending on the winery and the wines you taste, tasting costs might range from €10 to €50 or more.

**5. Activities: Burgundy provides a variety of activities, including outdoor experiences and trips to historical sites. Museum and attraction entrance prices normally vary from €5 to €15 per person.

**6. Budget for souvenirs, shopping, and unforeseen costs, among other miscellaneous expenses.

**7. Make sure you are knowledgeable about exchange rates and any possible costs for currency exchange or ATM withdrawals.

8. Travel Insurance: Take into account the price of comprehensive travel insurance, which can offer comfort in the event of unforeseen circumstances.

Keep in mind that your spending plan may change significantly depending on your travel preferences, length of stay, and travel style. It's a good idea to make a thorough financial plan to assist you in keeping track of your spending while you're in Burgundy.

2.5 Packing Essentials

It's important to carefully examine the temperature, activities, and cultural experiences of Burgundy when choosing your travel attire. The following list of things to bring for your trip is a guide:

1. Clothes: **Because Burgundy has different seasons, pack appropriately. Bring lightweight clothing, comfy walking shoes, and swimwear if you intend to make use of the lakes or canals in the spring and summer. carry layers for cooler temperatures in the fall, and in the winter, carry warm gear, such as a thick coat and gloves.

**2. Wearing comfortable walking shoes is essential whether you're touring old cities, vineyards, or the Morvan Natural Park. Verify that they are appropriate for the activities you have in mind.

**3. Electrical Adapters and Converters: France uses two-pin plugs of the Type C and Type E standard. If your equipment is incompatible with the European electrical system, be sure to pack the required voltage converters and adapters.

**4. Passports, visas, travel insurance, and any essential bookings or confirmations should all be kept in a safe, easily accessible location.

**5. medicine: If you take prescription medicine, make sure to bring enough of them along with any required paperwork. A simple first-aid kit is a smart idea as well.

**6. A compact backpack is excellent for day travel and carrying necessities like water, snacks, and extra clothes.

**7. Drink plenty of water while exploring by using a reusable bottle. Reusable bottles are both environmentally beneficial because clean drinking water is widely available.

**8. Although English is the primary language in Burgundy, having a language guide or translation software can be useful for conversation.

**9. Adaptable Clothing: Because the weather in Burgundy is unpredictable, accessories like scarves and light rain jackets can be beneficial.

**10. Bring enough cash in euros, and if you want to use credit or debit cards, let your bank know of your travel arrangements. There are many ATMs in use.

**11. To protect your belongings and luggage, use a travel lock.

**12. Books, e-readers, and other forms of entertainment for your free time while traveling.

Keep in mind to pack lightly so you may manage your luggage better while touring Burgundy. Burgundy is a beautiful place to travel because of its pleasant atmosphere, stunning landscapes, and diverse cultural experiences. You may be sure you're ready for all the thrills and discoveries waiting for you in this magical place by packing appropriately.

3. Gastronomic Treats And Beverages

3.1 Examining Burgundy's Gastronomic Traditions

East-central France's Burgundy is renowned for its thriving culinary scene. In addition to its own distinctive history and traditions, the region's cuisine is influenced by its closeness to Germany and Switzerland. Coq au vin, escargots, and boeuf bourguignon are some of the most well-liked foods in Burgundy. Additionally, the area is home to several well-known cheese producers, including Comté and Époisses de Bourgogne.

You can conduct the following activities to learn more about Burgundy's culinary traditions:

1. Visit a local market. This is one of the finest methods to learn about Burgundy's food culture. In most of the region's towns and villages, markets are held. Fresh

produce, cheese, meat, and other regional goods can be found in the markets.

2. Visit a winery. Burgundy is home to some of the most renowned wineries in the world. Tours and tastings are available at many wineries. This is a fantastic chance to learn about Burgundy's winemaking history and to try some of the best bottles produced there.

3. Visit a cheese shop. Several well-known cheesemakers are based in Burgundy. Burgundian cheese can be purchased and sampled at several cheese stores spread around the area.

4. Visit a restaurant. Both in the city and the countryside, Burgundy is home to several top-notch eateries. Make sure to sample some of the region's traditional foods, like escargots, boeuf bourguignon, and coq au vin.

Explore the Burgundy food and drink scene whether you're a foodie or just want to appreciate the region's distinctive culture. You won't be let down

Burgundy is a lovely region with a rich culinary culture that is ideal for exploring and enjoying food and drink.

3.2 Customary Burgundian Food

The eastern French province of Burgundy is well-known for its thriving culinary scene. In addition to its own distinctive history and traditions, the region's cuisine is influenced by its closeness to Germany and Switzerland.

Some of the most popular recipes and ingredients in Burgundy are listed below:

1. Coq au vin, a traditional Burgundian dish of braised chicken with mushrooms, bacon, and onions.

2. Escargots are cooked snails in butter, garlic, and parsley.

3. Beef bourguignon is a beef stew made with vegetables, herbs, and red wine.

4. Small, savory pastries made with choux dough and cheese are known as gougères.

5. A molded ham terrine cooked with parsley, garlic, and white wine is called a "jambon persillé."

6. Trout that has been dredged in flour and pan-fried in butter is known as "truite meunière."

3.2.1 Desserts from Burgundy

Burgundy is renowned not only for its traditional cuisine but also for its delectable pastries and desserts. Among the most well-liked sweets in Burgundy are:

1. Gingerbread, or pain d'épices
2. Crème brûlée, a custard with a crust made of caramelized sugar.
3. Tarte Tatin (apple tart turned upside down)
4. Small, spherical cookies prepared with almond flour are known as macarons.

3.2.2 Burgundian cheeses

Several well-known cheesemakers from around the world are based in Burgundy. Among the most well-liked cheeses from Burgundy are:

1. A strong, pungent cow's milk cheese called "Époisses de Bourgogne."
2. Comté: A firm, nutty cheese made from cow's milk.
3. A smooth, creamy cheese made from cow's milk.
4. Cîteaux: A cow's milk cheese with scrubbed rind.

Burgundian food is renowned for its use of seasonal, fresh ingredients. Numerous productive agricultural areas in the area provide a wide range of fruits, vegetables, and meats.

3.2.3 Typical Ingredients from Burgundy

Burgundian cuisine frequently uses the following ingredients:

1. meat: Burgundy is well-known for its premium meat. Typically, pasture-raised beef from Burgundy is fed a natural diet.

2. Pork is another common element in Burgundian cuisine. Pork from Burgundy is frequently grown on pasture and provides a natural diet.

3. Chicken: Burgundian cuisine frequently uses chicken as an element. Typically, pasture-raised chicken from Burgundy is fed a natural diet.

4. Mushrooms: A variety of wild mushrooms may be found in Burgundy and are frequently utilized in local dishes. The chanterelles, morels, and truffles are some of Burgundy's most well-known wild mushrooms.

5. Wines: Burgundy is home to some of the most renowned wine regions in the world. Burgundian cuisine frequently uses wines from the region to enhance the flavor of meals.

6. Cheeses: Several well-known cheese producers are based in Burgundy. Cheeses from Burgundy are frequently offered as a dessert or a snack.

There are a few things you may do if you want to try some typical Burgundian dishes:

1. Visit a neighborhood market. This is one of the greatest ways to sample Burgundian food. In most of the region's towns and villages, markets are held. Fresh produce, cheese, meat, and other regional goods can be found in the markets.

2. Visit a restaurant. Both in the city and the countryside, Burgundy is home to several top-notch eateries. Make sure to sample some of the region's traditional foods, like escargots, boeuf bourguignon, and coq au vin.

3. Prepare meals at home. If you're feeling daring, you may try preparing some classic Burgundian foods. Online and in cookbooks, there are a lot of recipes to choose from.

You're guaranteed to savor the mouthwatering food and drink of the area, regardless of how you decide to taste Burgundian cuisine.

3.3 Local Grocery Stores and Dining Out

The eastern French province of Burgundy is well-known for its thriving culinary scene. There are many top-notch local food markets and dining options in the area.

Local grocery stores

A trip to a neighborhood market is among the best ways to explore Burgundy's culinary tradition. In most of the region's towns and villages, markets are held. Fresh produce, cheese, meat, and other regional goods can be found in the markets.

In Burgundy, some of the most well-known regional food markets are:

1. One of the biggest and most well-known food markets in Burgundy is Les Halles de Dijon, a covered market in Dijon. The market is open from Tuesday through Saturday and has a huge selection of merchants selling local goods such as fresh meat, cheese, and veggies.

2. The Marché de Beaune is a market that takes place every Wednesday and Saturday in Beaune. There are numerous merchants at the market selling local goods such as fresh produce, cheese, and meat.

3. Marché de Mâcon: Every Saturday is market day in Mâcon. There are numerous merchants at the market selling local goods such as fresh produce, cheese, and meat.

4. Marché de Chagny: This market is held each Sunday in Chagny. There are numerous merchants at the market selling local goods such as fresh produce, cheese, and meat.

Food-related experiences

Burgundy provides a variety of culinary experiences in addition to local markets for food. These can include food excursions, wine tastings, and cooking workshops.

In Burgundy, some of the most well-liked gastronomic experiences are:

1. Cooking classes: Burgundy is home to a variety of cooking schools that provide cooking lessons. You can learn how to prepare some of Burgundy's most well-known meals, like boeuf bourguignon, escargots, and coq au vin.

2. Wine tastings: Burgundy is home to some of the most well-known wine areas in the world. Burgundy has many wineries that provide wine sampling. This is a fantastic chance to learn about Burgundy's winemaking history and to try some of the best bottles produced there.

3. several organizations in Burgundy provide cuisine tours. These excursions can take you to some of the top eateries, marketplaces, and wineries in the area.

You're sure to find a gastronomic experience in Burgundy that you'll appreciate, no matter what your hobbies or budget are.

3.4 Wine Types and Visits to Vineyards

The eastern French region of Burgundy is well-known for its top-notch wines. Numerous wine grape varieties, including Pinot Noir, Chardonnay, Gamay, Sauvignon Blanc, and Aligoté, are grown in the area.

1. Pinot Noir: Burgundy's most well-known wine grape variety is Pinot Noir. Red wines made from the grape variety Pinot Noir are prized for their refinement, grace, and complexity. Burgundian Pinot Noir wines can be delicate and fruity or full-bodied and substantial.

2. The second most well-known wine grape variety in Burgundy is Chardonnay. White wines made from the Chardonnay grape variety are renowned for their minerality, richness, and complexity. Burgundian Chardonnay wines can be anything from delicate and crisp to full-bodied and creamy.

3. Gamay is a red grape varietal famous for producing delicious and approachable wines. The main grape used to make Beaujolais wine is called gamay. However, some red wines in Burgundy are also made with the Gamay grape.

4. Sauvignon Blanc is a white grape variety that produces wines that are crisp and energizing. Despite not being as frequently planted in Burgundy as Pinot Noir or Chardonnay, Sauvignon Blanc is nonetheless used to make some of the region's best wines.

5. White grape varietal **Aligoté**: Aligoté is renowned for its high acidity and minerality. Despite not having the same popularity as Pinot Noir or Chardonnay,

aligoté is utilized to make some exceptional wines in Burgundy, particularly in the Chablis region.

<u>Vinyard Excursions</u>

Visits to vineyards are among the greatest ways to learn about Burgundy wine. In Burgundy, numerous vineyards provide tours and tastings. This is a fantastic way to learn about the area's winemaking history and to try some of the greatest wines produced there.

Here are a few of Burgundy's most well-known vineyards:

1. "Domaine de la Romanée-Conti": This vineyard is renowned for creating some of the priciest and most sought-after wines in the world.

2. The vineyard known as **Domaine Armand Rousseau** is renowned for producing some of Burgundy's finest Pinot Noir wines.

3. The vineyard known as Domaine Leflaive is renowned for producing some of Burgundy's finest Chardonnay wines.

4. The vineyard known as Domaine Coche-Dury is renowned for producing some of Burgundy's finest white wines.

I strongly advise going to a vineyard if you want to understand more about Burgundy's wine. It is a fantastic way to learn about the area's winemaking history and to try some of the greatest wines produced there.

3.5 Beer and Other Regional Drinks

In addition to producing some of the best brewers and distilleries in the world, Burgundy is also known for its world-class wines.

A. **Beer**

Bière de Bourgogne is the most widely consumed beer in Burgundy. The pale brew Bière de Bourgogne has a malty flavor and a slightly bitter aftertaste. Typically fermented in oak barrels, bière de Bourgogne has a distinct flavor profile.

Burgundy's other well-liked beer varieties include:

1. Bière de Garde, an amber ale with a rich flavor profile and a lingering finish. Typically, bière de garde is made in the winter and matured until spring or summer.

2. Bière Blanche: Bière Blanche is a hazy wheat beer with a flavor that is delightful. Typically, coriander and orange peel are used in the brewing process of bière blanche.

3. Bière Blonde is a light beer with a crisp aftertaste and a clean flavor. In France, Bière Blonde is the most often consumed beer style.

4. Bière Brune is a black lager with a full flavor and a silky finish. Roasted malts are commonly used in the

brewing of bière brune, giving it its dark color and robust flavor.

B. Additional Local Beverages

Burgundy is the home to several regional drinks in addition to beer. These drinks consist of:

1. Crème de Cassis: Made in Burgundy, Crème de Cassis is a liqueur made from black currants. The common ingredient in Kir, a popular aperitif in France, is crème de cassis.

2. Pastis: Produced in Burgundy, pastis is an anise-flavored liqueur. Pastis is often served with ice and water as a dilution.

3. Dijon mustard is a particular variety of mustard made in Dijon, the city of Burgundy. Dijon mustard is renowned for its strong flavor and sinus-clearing properties.

4. Burgundy is home to a variety of natural springs that provide top-notch mineral water. Burgundy is known for its love of mineral water, which is frequently offered with meals.

Where to Drink Local Beer and Other Drinks in Burgundy

In Burgundy, there are several locations where you can sample beer and other regional drinks. These locations comprise:

1. Breweries: Tours and tastings are available at numerous breweries in Burgundy. This is a fantastic way to discover more about the area's brewing heritage and to try some of its best brews.

2. Bars: There are a lot of bars in Burgundy that serve a selection of regional beers and other drinks.

3. Burgundy has a large number of eateries that serve regional beers and other alcoholic beverages.

4. Burgundy has a lot of food stalls where you can get local beer and other drinks.

Burgundy is the ideal location to drink a beer or other regional beverage because of its storied brewing history and stunning landscape.

4. Dining And Nightlife

4.1 Restaurants in Burgundy

The eastern French province of Burgundy is well-known for its delectable gastronomy and outstanding wines. From Michelin-starred restaurants to laid-back bistros, the region's eateries provide a variety of dining alternatives.

Here are a few of Burgundy's top restaurants:

1. La Côte Saint-Jacques in Joigny, which has a Michelin star, serves a tasting menu of contemporary French cuisine produced with local, seasonal ingredients.

2. * **Ma Cuisine:** This Beaune restaurant gives a unique twist on typical Burgundian fare.

3. * **Le Pré Catelan:** This Dijon eatery serves you traditional French fare in a chic environment.

4. * **La Closerie:** This lovely Beaune restaurant serves you authentic Burgundian cuisine.

5. * **Le Bistrot du Clos:** This Beaune eatery provides a relaxed and inexpensive eating experience with an emphasis on seasonal ingredients.

You may enjoy a tasty lunch at one of Burgundy's many restaurants no matter your taste or budget.

4.2 Fine Dining Establishments and Establishments with Michelin stars

The eastern French province of Burgundy is well-known for its delectable gastronomy and outstanding wines. Numerous Michelin-starred restaurants and great gourmet eateries can be found in the area, offering a range of eating options from traditional French fare to contemporary takes on Burgundian specialties.

Here are some of Burgundy's top fine dining places and Michelin-starred eateries:

1. La Côte Saint-Jacques (Joigny): With three Michelin stars, this eatery serves seasonal modern French cuisine on a tasting menu. By the Yonne River, the restaurant is situated in a stunning environment.

2. The Michelin-three-starred restaurant **Maison Lameloise** (Chagny) serves a tasting menu of traditional French cuisine with a contemporary twist. The restaurant is situated in the middle of the Burgundy wine region, in a quaint town.

3. * **William Frachot** (Dijon): With two Michelin stars, this establishment serves up a tasting menu of contemporary French food crafted with seasonal, local ingredients. In the center of Dijon, the restaurant is situated in a chic environment.

4. * **Loiseau des Ducs** (Dijon): This Michelin-starred restaurant serves traditional French fare with a contemporary twist. In the center of Dijon, the restaurant is housed in a historic mansion.

5. * **Pré Catelan** (Dijon): This Michelin-starred establishment serves a tasting menu of traditional French fare with an emphasis on fresh ingredients. The restaurant is situated beside the Lac Kir in a lovely area.

6. * **Bernard Loiseau:** This restaurant in Saulieu, France, has two Michelin stars. The eatery serves a tasting menu of traditional French fare.

7. The two-star L'Espérance restaurant is situated in Saint-Père-en-Retz, France. A modern French tasting menu is available at the restaurant.

8. * **L'Ambroisie:** This two-Michelin-star Dijon eatery serves a tasting menu of contemporary French cuisine produced with ingredients that are obtained locally. The restaurant has a comfortable eating area with exposed beams and stone walls that are housed in a charming 18th-century structure.

9. * **Ma Cuisine:** This Beaune restaurant with a Michelin star provides inventive twists on classic Burgundian fare. The eatery, housed in a former

16th-century manor, has a chic dining area with exposed stone walls and contemporary furnishings.

4.3 Rneighborhood Bistros and Classic Restaurants

The eastern French province of Burgundy is well-known for its delectable gastronomy and outstanding wines. Additionally, the area is home to some top-notch neighborhood bistros and classic restaurants that provide a more relaxed and inexpensive dining experience.

Here are a few of Burgundy's top neighborhood bistros and classic restaurants:

1. Le Bouchon des Filles (Beaune): This quaint cafe serves traditional French cuisine. Escargots, boeuf bourguignon, and coq au vin are a few of the most well-liked delicacies.

2. Traditional Burgundian dishes prepared with Dijon mustard are available on the menu at Le Bistrot de la

Moutarde in Dijon. The crème brûlée, boeuf bourguignon, and jambon persillé are among of the most well-liked delicacies.

3. * **Le Bouchon des Prés** (Dijon): This vibrant bistro serves up a menu of classic Burgundian fare. Escargots, boeuf bourguignon, and tarte tatin are some of the most well-liked foods.

4. * **Le Bistrot du Parc** (Dijon): Located next to a park, this café serves up classic Burgundian fare. Escargots, crème brûlée, and coq au vin are a few of the most well-liked delicacies.

5. * **Chez Nous** (Dijon): This typical Burgundian eatery features a menu of traditional meals prepared using seasonal, fresh ingredients. Escargots, boeuf bourguignon, and coq au vin are a few of the most well-liked delicacies.

6. Le Cellier aux Moines is a cafe in the French town of Vézelay. Traditional Burgundian fare like coq au vin and boeuf bourguignon are served at the bistro.

7. This restaurant is situated in Beaune, France, says Chez Paul. French classics like steak frites and moules frites are served at the bistro.

8. Le Bistro du Palais is a restaurant in the French city of Dijon. Both conventional Burgundian fare and contemporary French cuisine are offered at the bistro.

These are just a few of Burgundy's many top-notch neighborhood bistros and classic restaurants. Check out one of these eateries if you want a more relaxed and reasonably priced dining experience.

4.4 Wine Shops and Wineries

Eastern France's Burgundy is known across the world for its wine. Some of the most prominent wine estates in the world, including Romanée-Conti and Domaine de la

Romanée-Conti, are found in the area. In addition, there are several top-notch wine cellars and pubs in Burgundy, which make it easy to try some of the best wines produced there.

Here are a few of Burgundy's top wineries and bars:

1. La Cave des Grands Crus (Beaune): A large variety of Burgundian wines, many from renowned growers, are available at this wine bar and vault. Burgundian wine-tasting menus are also available at the bar.

2. Burgundian wines, as well as wines from other parts of France and the world, are available in large quantities at the wine bar and cellar known as La Cave du Roy in the city of Macon. Burgundian wine-tasting menus are also available at the bar.

3. The Vougeot wine region's Le Clos de Vougeot wine bar and cellar is situated right in the middle of it. Numerous Burgundian wines, as well as wines from other parts of France and the globe, are available at the

bar. Burgundian wine-tasting menus are also available at the bar.

4. Dijon's **La Part des Anges** wine bar and cellar features a sizable collection of Burgundian wines in addition to those from other parts of France and the globe. Burgundian wine-tasting menus are also available at the bar.

5. * **Chez Nous** (Dijon): This classic Burgundian eatery boasts a wine bar and cellar as well. Numerous Burgundian wines, as well as wines from other parts of France and the globe, are available at the bar.

Cafes

Additionally, there are numerous cafes throughout Burgundy. Cafes are informal dining establishments that offer small meals and snacks. The following are some of Burgundy's most well-known cafes:

1. The Cafe des Arts, which is situated in Dijon, France. The cafe offers coffee, snacks, and small meals.

2. Cafe de la Poste: This restaurant is situated in Beaune, France. The cafe offers coffee, snacks, and small meals.

3. Café de la Place: This café is situated in the French town of Vézelay. The cafe offers coffee, snacks, and small meals.

These are only a few of Burgundy's many top-notch wine bars and cellars. If you enjoy wine, make sure to visit one of these locations while you are in the area.

4.5 Places for Entertainment and Nightlife

Additionally, the area is home to several top-notch nightlife and entertainment spots that provide a wide range of options for guests of all ages and interests.

4.5.1 Nightclubs

Many great nightclubs in Burgundy include a range of musical styles and settings. In Burgundy, some of the most well-known nightclubs are:

1.* **Le République** (Dijon): Burgundy's biggest and most well-known nightclub. Hip-hop, R&B, and electronic music are among the musical styles available.

2. * **La Cave du Roy** (Mâcon): Located in the center of Mâcon, this club plays a range of musical styles, including house, techno, and trance.

3. The nightclub Le Clos de Vougeot (Vougeot) is situated in the heart of the Burgundy wine region and features a range of musical styles, including hip-hop, R&B, and electronic music.

4.5.2 Bars and Pubs

The superb bars and pubs in Burgundy also provide a more laid-back and informal vibe than nightclubs. The following are a few of the most well-liked taverns and pubs in Burgundy:

1. Le Bouchon des Filles (Beaune): This pub serves a large variety of wines, beers, and cocktails in a traditional French setting.

2. Dijon's *Le Bistrot de la Moutarde* offers a wide variety of wines, beers, and drinks in a classic Burgundian setting.

3. * **Le Bouchon des Prés** (Dijon): This pub features a buzzing ambiance and a large variety of wines, beers, and cocktails.

4.5.3 Live Music Locations

Additionally, Burgundy is home to many top-notch live music venues that play a range of musical styles, including jazz, blues, and rock. In Burgundy, some of the most well-liked live music venues are:

1. *La Cave des Grands Crus (Beaune): This venue has jazz, blues, and rock concerts among other live music genres.

2. * **La Part des Anges** (Dijon): This venue hosts jazz, blues, and rock concerts among other live music genres.

3. * **Chez Nous** (Dijon): This venue has jazz, blues, and rock performances among other live music genres.

4.5.4 Additional Entertainment Locations

Burgundy has a variety of additional entertainment places in addition to nightclubs, bars, pubs, and live music venues, including:

1. Casinos: Burgundy is home to several casinos that provide a selection of gambling games like slots, table games, and poker.

2. * **Movie Theaters:** Burgundy is home to a handful of theaters that show both new and vintage movies.

3. Burgundy is home to a variety of bowling alleys, which provide an enjoyable activity for families and groups of friends.

4. Burgundy is home to several arcades that provide a selection of video games and other arcade games.

Burgundy boasts a wide variety of nightlife and entertainment options, so there is something for everyone. Burgundy is the perfect place to discover a night out on the town, a laid-back evening at a pub, or a live music event.

5. Shopping In Burgundy

5.1 Burgundy Retail Therapy

The eastern French province of Burgundy is famed for its delectable gastronomy, world-class wines, and picturesque landscapes. Luxury boutiques and lovely antique stores are among the region's many fantastic shopping options.

Here are a few spots to visit in Burgundy if you're seeking to indulge in some shopping therapy:

A. **Dijon**

Burgundy's city, Dijon, offers a wide range of shopping opportunities, including high-end shops and department stores. The following are some of Dijon's top shopping destinations:

1.* "Rue de la Liberté" is a pedestrian-only street dotted with stores offering everything from food and housewares to clothing and accessories.

2. * **La Place de la Libération:** This bustling area is dotted with stores, cafes, and eateries.

3. * **Le Centre Commercial de la Toison d'Or:** This cutting-edge mall is home to numerous domestic and foreign brands.

B. **Beaune**

In the center of the Burgundy wine region sits the lovely town of Beaune. There are several shops in the town that sell goods from the area, including wine, cheese, and mustard. The following are some of the top stores in Beaune:

4. * **Rue Coquard:** This small street is lined with boutiques that market cheese, wine, and other regional goods.

5. * **La Place Carnot:** This bustling area is dotted with stores, cafes, and eateries.

6. * **Les Halles de Beaune:** This covered market is home to numerous sellers offering local goods like fresh produce, cheese, and meat.

7.* **Boutique La Cave:** This store offers a selection of clothing and accessories for both men and women from French and worldwide brands.

8. * **Boutique L'Atelier du Verre:** This store offers a selection of handcrafted jewelry and accessories made of glass.

C. Other Burgundy Towns and Villages

Other cities and villages in Burgundy, like Dijon and Beaune, also provide fantastic shopping options. The following are some of the top stores in Burgundy:

7. * **Chagny:** Several shops in this quaint village sell goods from the area, including ceramics, wine, and cheese.

8. * Semur-en-Auxois: This historic village is home to several boutiques and antique stores that sell regional goods.

9. * **Vézelay:** This hilltop village is the location of several businesses that market regional goods including wine, cheese, and lavender.

Burgundy Shopping Advice

Following are some suggestions for shopping in Burgundy:

-* Be ready to pay more: Burgundy is a region with a high cost of living, so be ready to pay more for products and services.

- * **Look for regional products:** Burgundy is the source of a variety of top-notch regional goods, including wine, cheese, and mustard. When you shop, be sure to look for these items.

-* **Don't be scared to bargain:** In marketplaces and tiny stores in Burgundy, haggling is popular.

- Enjoy the experience: Shopping in Burgundy is a wonderful way to learn about the customs and culture of the area. Take your time, and delight in the experience.

Burgundy has a wide variety of shopping possibilities, so it has something for everyone. Burgundy is the perfect place to shop for anything you need, from new clothing to a travel memento or a present for a friend.

5.2 Local Artists' Workshops and Crafts

Burgundy is also home to several local artisan stores and workshops where you can get one-of-a-kind handmade goods and learn about the area's traditional skills.

Here are some of Burgundy's most well-known local artisan businesses and workshops:

1. **Pottery**: Burgundy has a long tradition of producing pottery, and the area is home to several potteries where you can buy handcrafted wares or even enroll in a pottery lesson. In Burgundy, some of the most well-known potteries are:

-* Beaune's Poterie de Bourgogne
-* Chagny's Atelier du Verre
-* Nuits-Saint-Georges' Poterie de Nuits-Saint-Georges
-* Saint-Aignan's Poterie de Saint-Aignan

2. Another well-liked art in Burgundy is **glassblowing,** and the area is home to several glassblowing studios where you can buy handcrafted glass objects or even enroll in a glassblowing course. The following are a few of the most well-known glassblowing studios in Burgundy:

- * Chagny's Atelier du Verre
-* Chevannes' La Verrerie Ouvrière de Bourgogne
-* Passavant-la-Rochère's Verrerie La Rochère

3. * **Blacksmithing:** There are many blacksmiths in the area where you may buy handcrafted ironwork products or even enroll in a blacksmithing lesson. Blacksmithing is a traditional craft in Burgundy. In Burgundy, some of the most well-known blacksmiths are:

-* Semur-en-Auxois' La Forge de Semur
-* Beaune's La Forge d'Auxois
-* Dijon's La Forge de Bourgogne

4. * **Tapestry weaving:** There are several tapestry workshops in the area where you may buy handcrafted tapestries or even enroll in a tapestry weaving lesson. Tapestry weaving is a traditional craft in Burgundy. In Burgundy, some of the most well-known tapestry studios are:

-* Vézelay's La Maison de la Tapisserie
-* Aubusson's Atelier de Tapisserie d'Aubusson
*- Felletin's Atelier de Tapisserie de Felletin

In addition to these particular crafts, Burgundy is home to a variety of other local artisan stores where you may buy handcrafted things like jewelry, apparel, and housewares.

5.3 Vintage Shops and Antique Stores

There are many great antique shops and vintage finds in the area where you can locate one-of-a-kind and exquisite artifacts from the past.

Here are a handful of Burgundy's top vintage shops and antique shops:

1. *Brocante de Beaune** (Beaune): Every Sunday morning, this sizable antique market offers a wide range of antique and vintage things, including furniture, clothing, and household goods.

2. * **Le Grenier de Chagny** (Chagny): Housed in a charming 18th-century structure, this antique shop sells a

wide range of antique and vintage antiques, including furniture, paintings, and decorative objects.

3. * **La Puce de Dijon** (Dijon): This flea market offers a wide range of antique and vintage objects, including clothing, furniture, and books. It is held every Sunday morning.

4. * **Brocante de Semur** (Semur-en-Auxois): This flea market sells a wide range of antique and vintage products, including furniture, clothing, and home goods. It is held every Sunday afternoon.

5. * **Le Grenier de Vézelay** (Vézelay): This antique shop is situated in the hilltop village of Vézelay and has a large selection of vintage and antique antiques, including furniture, paintings, and decorative objects.

In addition to these particular shops and fairs, Burgundy is home to a lot of other fantastic antique shops and vintage treasures. Investigate the nearby little towns and villages to discover the finest bargains.

5.4 Local Goods and Souvenirs

Burgundy is also the source of many top-notch local goods and souvenirs. Here are some of the most well-liked Burgundian goods and souvenirs:

1. Wine: Burgundy is the birthplace of some of the most renowned winemakers in the world, including Romanée-Conti and Domaine de la Romanée-Conti. A bottle of Burgundian wine makes the ideal memento of your journey.

2. * Mustard: Dijon is the Burgundy's capital and is famous for its Dijon mustard. Dijon mustard is a robust, aromatic condiment produced from black mustard seeds and white wine. It is a staple in French cooking and is used to create sauces, marinades, and salad dressings.

3. Époisses de Bourgogne, Brillat-Savarin, and Citeaux are just a few of the outstanding cheeses that can be found in Burgundy. The fresh milk from the cows and goats in the area is used to make these cheeses. They are

often matured for a few weeks or months, giving them a flavorful complexity.

4. Honey: Several beekeepers in Burgundy make honey from the area's wildflowers. Honey from Burgundy is renowned for its flavor and scent. It is a widely used component in French cooking and is used to make sauces, sweets, and pastries.

5. Burgundy has a long history of producing pottery. Many potters in the area specialize in producing one-of-a-kind, handmade ceramics. Pottery from Burgundy is a well-liked memento of travel.

6. Glassware: Another specialty of Burgundy is glassware. You can buy handcrafted glass objects in the area from one of the many glassblowing workshops. Glassware in the color burgundy is a preferred travel keepsake.

There are many other top-notch souvenirs and regional goods that you can buy in Burgundy in addition to these particular keepsakes. For the greatest prices, make sure to investigate the nearby villages and small towns.

Regions of Burgundy

6. Côte-d'Or

The department of **Côte-d'Or** is located in eastern France's Bourgogne-Franche-Comté region. It is renowned for its exquisite cuisine, acclaimed wines, and picturesque surroundings. Dijon, the department's main city, serves as the Côte-d'Or's capital.

6.1 **Dijon**

A wonderful city with a deep history and culture is Dijon. Numerous palaces, cathedrals, and other important historical sites can be found throughout the city.

6.1.1 "Castles and Palaces"

1. Palais des Ducs et des États de Bourgogne: The Dukes of Burgundy used to reside in this palace. It presently

serves as a museum and has a collection of works of art and historical objects from the area.

2. * The Cathedral Saint-Bénigne in Dijon is a magnificent example of Romanesque and Gothic architecture. It is among France's most magnificent churches.

3. * **Église Notre-Dame de Dijon:** This church is renowned for its stunning stained glass windows and Gothic architecture.

6.1.2 Must Visit Historic Locations

1. *Dijon's Musée des Beaux-Arts, which exhibits a collection of artwork dating from the Middle Ages to the present.

2. * **Musée Magnin:** This museum is home to a collection of artwork from the 19th century.

3. François Rude, a French artist, is the subject of this museum, which is devoted to his life and creative output.

4. This tower is a piece of the old city fortifications, the Tour Philippe le Bon. It offers breathtaking city views.

5. Another relic of the medieval city walls is the Porte Guillaume. One of Dijon's most recognizable landmarks is it.

Other Important Historical Locations in the Côte-d'Or

-* The *Abbaye de Fontenay* is a UNESCO World Heritage Site. It is one of France's most well-preserved Cistercian abbeys.

-* The Burgundy wine region's *Château de Clos Vougeot* is where you'll find this castle. Wine aficionados frequently travel there.

-* The former residence of the French author Roger de Bussy-Rabutin was the **Château de Bussy-Rabutin**. It presently serves as a museum and contains a collection of furnishings, artwork, and other relics from the 17th century.

6.1.3 Museums and galleries of fine art

1. *Dijon's Musée des Beaux-Arts, which exhibits a collection of artwork dating from the Middle Ages to the present.

2. Musée Magnin: This museum is home to a collection of artwork from the 19th century.

3. François Rude, a French artist, is the subject of this museum, which is devoted to his life and creative output.

4. *Musée Consortium: This contemporary art gallery hosts cutting-edge and thought-provoking shows by French and international artists.

5. The Burgundian people's history from the 18th to the 20th centuries is depicted in this museum, the Musée de la Vie Bourguignonne.

6. The museum that holds this collection of religious artwork spans the Middle Ages to the present.

7. Musée de l'Homme: This museum chronicles the development and culture of humanity.

8. The owls throughout the world are the focus of this museum, which is called the Musée de la Chouette.

9. Musée de la Moutarde: This museum chronicles the history of Dijon's mustard production.

10. "Musée du Pain d'Épices": This museum chronicles the history of Dijon's gingerbread production.

11. Burgundy's winemaking history is chronicled in this museum, the Musée du Vin de Bourgogne.

6.1.4 Gardens and Parks:

1. Dijon's botanical garden, the Jardin des Plantes, is situated in the city's center. Many different kinds of plants from throughout the world reside there.
2. The Park of the Colombière is situated in the city of Dijon. It is a well-liked location for both locals and visitors to unwind and take in the outdoors.

3. In the city of Dijon, there is a park called the Parc de la Toison d'Or. There are many attractions there, such as a zoo, a playground, and a lake.

4. The heart of the Burgundy wine region is home to the **Jardin du Clos Vougeot**. There are many different kinds of flora there, such as roses, grapes, and lavender.

5. Bussy-le-Grand is home to the park known as the Château de Bussy-Rabutin. There are many attractions there, such as a lake, a playground, and a castle.

6.1.5 The Côte d'Or's natural landmarks include:

1. Regional Natural Park of Morvan: The Côte-d'Or's northern section is home to this regional natural park. Forests, lakes, and rivers are just a few of the natural wonders that may be found there.
2. The Tronçais Forest is situated in the southern portion of the Côte d'Or. It is one of France's biggest oak woodlands.

3. Lac de Saint-Point: This lake may be found in the Côte-d'Or's northern region. It is a well-liked location for boating, fishing, and swimming.

4. Cascade de Gouloux: This waterfall can be found in the Côte-d'Or's northern region. It is one of France's tallest waterfalls.

6.1.6 Côte-d'Or Markets and Shopping:

1. The centre of Dijon is home to this covered market, known as Les Halles de Dijon. There are numerous

vendors there who sell local goods including fresh produce, pork, and cheese.

2. Rue de la Liberté: This pedestrian-only strip is dotted with stores offering everything from home furnishings and cuisine to clothing and accessories.

3. Brocante de Beaune: This flea market for antiques is held in Beaune every Sunday. It is a fantastic location to discover unusual and one-of-a-kind goods.

4. Marché de Semur-en-Auxois: This market is held in Semur-en-Auxois every Tuesday morning. It is a fantastic location to find local goods like cheese and fresh veggies.

5. Every Sunday morning in Vézelay, there is a market called the Marché de Vézelay. It is a fantastic location to find local goods like cheese and fresh veggies.

6.2 Beaune

6.2.1 "Beaune - History and Wine"

In the center of the Burgundy wine region sits the lovely town of Beaune. It is renowned for its exquisite cuisine, acclaimed wines, and picturesque surroundings. The Hospices de Beaune, a UNESCO World Heritage Site, and other historical sites may be found in Beaune.

The history of Beaune goes all the way back to the Roman era. In the 13th century, the town was fortified and developed into a major trading and commercial hub. Beaune was chosen as the dukes of Burgundy's seat of government in the fifteenth century. The town went through a period of considerable wealth during this time, and many of its most significant historical structures were built.

The famed wines of Beaune are well-known worldwide. Romanée-Conti and La Tâche are two of the most costly and sought-after wines in the world, and vines that make them are all around the town. Numerous wine shops and auction houses may be found in Beaune.

In 1443, the Hospices de Beaune, a medieval hospital and hospice, was established. Nicolas Rolin, the chancellor of the dukes of Burgundy, constructed the hospital. One of the top tourist destinations in Beaune is the Hospices de Beaune, a UNESCO World Heritage Site.

Care for the aged and sick is provided by the Hospices de Beaune, which is still in business today. A museum with a collection of artwork and memorabilia from the hospital's past is also located within the facility.

6.2.2 Hospices of Beaune

Nicolas Rolin, the chancellor of the Duke of Burgundy, established the Hospices de Beaune, a medieval hospital, in 1443. To provide care for the sick and underprivileged, the hospital was constructed.

Now a museum and wine auction house, Hospices de Beaune. A variety of artwork and historical objects from the hospital are on display in the museum. Some of the most costly wines in the world are auctioned off by the wine auction house.

One of Burgundy's most visited tourist destinations is the Hospices de Beaune. For everyone who likes wine or history, it is a must-see.

6.2.3 Auction of Beaune Wines

Every November, the Beaune Wine Auction is conducted. One of the most significant wine auctions ever held takes place here.

Vineyard-produced wines from the Hospices de Beaune are sold at auction to the highest bidder. The Hospices de Beaune are supported with the money raised during the auction.

A prominent event that draws buyers from all around the world is the Beaune Wine Auction. The chance to sample and purchase some of the best wines in the world is fantastic.

Activities in Beaune include:

-* Go on a wine tour: Because Beaune is surrounded by vineyards, there are several wine tours available. Wine tours are a fantastic way to discover more about local wines and taste some of the best wines in the world.
-* Pay a visit to the Musée du Vin de Bourgogne: This museum chronicles the history of Burgundy's wine industry. The museum is an excellent site to discover the history of the area's winemaking practices and to taste some of the regional libations.

-* Go to the Basilique Notre-Dame de Beaune: The 13th-century Gothic basilica known as the Basilique Notre-Dame de Beaune is a must-see. Several significant works of art, including a polyptych by Rogier van der Weyden, may be seen inside the basilica.

-* Go to the Hôtel de Ville de Beaune: Constructed in the 16th century, this Renaissance town hall is a must-see. Numerous significant works of art, including a tapestry that portrays Saint Nicholas' life, may be found inside the town hall.

6.2.4 Cellars and Wine Tasting Experiences in Beaune

Some of the most renowned winemakers in the world call Beaune, a town in the heart of the Burgundy wine region, home. As a result, Beaune offers lots of chances for wine-sampling excursions and cellar visits.

Here are some of Beaune's most well-liked wineries and wine-tasting events:

1. *Maison Louis Jadot: This winery provides numerous wine sampling opportunities, such as a guided tour of the cellars and a tasting of various different wines.

2. * **Domaine Bouchard Père et Fils:** This winery provides a selection of wine-tasting experiences, such as

a guided tour of the cellars and a sampling of many distinctive wines.

3. * **Joseph Drouhin:** This winery provides a range of wine-tasting opportunities, including a tour of the cellars and a sampling of various distinct wines.

4. * **Patriarche Père et Fils:** This winery provides a range of wine-tasting experiences, including a tour of the cellars and a sample of several wines.
5. * **Albert Bichot:** This winery provides a range of wine-tasting experiences, including a tour of the cellars and a sample of numerous wines.

6. The wine bar and store **Caveau des Ducs de Bourgogne** provides a range of wine-tasting experiences, including samplings of various wines from the Burgundy area.

7. * **Caveau de la Moutarde Fallot:** This mustard shop and museum offers several mustard-tasting

opportunities, including samplings of various Burgundy-region mustards.

8. * **Caveau de la Chouette:** This wine bar and store provides a range of wine-tasting experiences, including samplings of various Burgundy wines.

9. * **Caveau de la Madeleine:** This wine bar and store provides a range of wine-tasting experiences, including samplings of various Burgundy wines.

10. * **Caveau de la Tour:** This wine bar and store provides a range of wine-tasting experiences, including samplings of various Burgundy wines.

11. * **Caveau de la Vigne:** This wine bar and store provides numerous wine-tasting opportunities, including samplings of various wines from the Burgundy region.

6.2.5 Historic Streets and Buildings

Beaune is a historic city with numerous well-preserved structures from the Renaissance and the Middle Ages. The town center is a labyrinth of little streets and passageways dotted with boutiques, eateries, and coffee shops.

In Beaune, some of the most notable historic streets and buildings are:

1. One of Beaune's most visited tourist destinations, the Hospices de Beaune, is located on Rue de l'Hôtel Dieu.
2. * **Place de la Halle:** Located in this square is the Beaune Market Hall, a covered market that offers local goods such as fresh vegetables, pork, and cheese.

3. The Collegiale Notre-Dame de Beaune is one of Burgundy's most significant religious structures and a Gothic masterpiece.

4. * **Hôtel de Ville de Beaune:** This town hall is a stunning Renaissance structure.

5. * Tour Philippe le Bon: This tower, which is a piece of the old city fortifications, provides breathtaking views over Beaune.

6. * **Porte Guillaume:** One of Beaune's most recognizable monuments, this gate is another reminder of the old city fortifications.

Everyone may find something to enjoy in the lovely and historic town of Beaune. You will have a great time in Beaune whether you are interested in wine, history, or culture.

6.3. Wine and Charm at Nuits-Saint-Georges

Located in the Côte de Nuits, a subregion of the Burgundy wine region, Nuits-Saint-Georges is a lovely town. It is renowned for its exquisite cuisine, acclaimed wines, and extensive history.

6.3.1 Wineries and wine cellars

Some of the most renowned wine producers in the world, including Domaine de la Romanée-Conti, Domaine Leroy, and Domaine Armand Rousseau, are based in

Nuits-Saint-Georges. The town is also home to several top-notch wine cellars where you can explore, learn about, and taste some of the finest wines produced in the area.

Here are some of Nuits-Saint-Georges' most well-known wineries:

1. Domaine de la Romanée-Conti: One of the most renowned wineries in the world. Numerous tastings and cellar tours are available, but reservations are required.

2. Another notable winery in Nuits-Saint-Georges is **Domaine Leroy**. Numerous tastings and cellar excursions are available, but they must also be scheduled in advance.

3. One other notable winery in Nuits-Saint-Georges is Domaine Armand Rousseau. Numerous tastings and cellar excursions are available, but they must also be scheduled in advance.

4. * **Domaine Bertagna:** This winery provides a selection of cellar tours and tastings in addition to a wine bar where you may sip some of their beverages.

5. * **Domaine de Montille:** This winery provides a selection of cellar tours and tastings in addition to a wine bar where you may sip some of their beverages.

6. * **Domaine Prieuré Roch:** This winery provides a selection of cellar tours and tastings in addition to a wine bar where you may sip some of their beverages.

6.3.2 Historic sites and monuments

Historic Nuits-Saint-Georges is home to a variety of well-preserved Renaissance and medieval structures. The town center is a labyrinth of little streets and passageways dotted with boutiques, eateries, and coffee shops.

In Nuits-Saint-Georges, some of the most noteworthy historical structures and locations are:

1. *Château de Nuits-Saint-Georges: The Dukes of Burgundy once called this fortress home. It was constructed in the thirteenth century. It presently serves as a museum and has a collection of works of art and historical items from the town.

2. * Église Saint-Symphorien: This 12th-century church is a gem of Romanesque architecture. It ranks among the most significant places of worship in the Côte de Nuits area.

3. * *Hôtel de Ville de Nuits-Saint-Georges: This town hall, a Renaissance structure with a lovely front, was constructed in the sixteenth century.

4. * **Tour Philippe le Bon**: This tower, which is a piece of the old city walls, provides breathtaking views of Nuits-Saint-Georges.

5. * **Porte Guillaume:** One of Nuits-Saint-Georges' most recognizable landmarks, this gate is another reminder of the old city fortifications.

6. * Hospices de Nuits-Saint-Georges: Originally a hospital, this building today houses a museum and a wine auction house. It was built in the thirteenth century.

6.3.3 Gastronomy and Local Cuisine in Nuits-Saint-Georges

In addition to having world-class wines, Nuits-Saint-Georges is home to a delectable and varied cuisine. Numerous top-notch eateries in the town serve both classic Burgundian fare and more contemporary, inventive cuisine.

The following are a few of the most well-liked regional cuisines in Nuits-Saint-Georges:

1. Coq au vin, a traditional Burgundian dish composed of chicken, bacon, mushrooms, onions, and red wine.

2. Escargots: Escargots are often served as an appetizer. They are cooked in garlic butter and parsley.

3. Beef bourguignon: This stew is created with beef, red wine, onions, and mushrooms.

4. Gougères: Choux pastry and Gruyère cheese are used to make these cheesy treats.

5. Pain d'épices: Flour, honey, and spices are used to make this gingerbread.

Several top-notch bakeries and patisseries can be found in Nuits-Saint-Georges where you can buy fresh bread, pastries, and cakes.

6.3.4 Nuits-Saint-Georges Local Festivals and Wine-Related Events

Numerous festivals and wine-related activities are held all year long in Nuits-Saint-Georges. The most well-liked occasions include:

1.* "Fête de la Vigne": This annual celebration of the grape harvest takes place in September.

2. * **Nuits-Saint-Georges Wine Festival:** This event, which takes place every November, comprises wine tastings from producers in Nuits-Saint-Georges and other regions of Burgundy.

3. Every year in November, the Nuits-Saint-Georges Wine Auction is conducted, including some of the most costly wines in the world.

4. * La Paulée de Meursault: This annual event, which takes place in January, involves wine tastings from the Côte de Beaune village of Meursault.

Visitors may find a variety of attractions in the bustling town of Nuits-Saint-Georges. You will have a great time at Nuits-Saint-Georges whether you are interested in wine, food, or culture.

6.4 Additional Cities and Towns

There are numerous other quaint towns and villages on the Côte-d'Or, each with its own distinct personality and attractions.

Here are some of the Côte-d'Or's most well-known cities and towns:

1. Semur-en-Auxois is a hilltop town renowned for its exquisite architecture and well-preserved medieval walls.

2. Flavigny-sur-Ozerain is a charming hamlet well-known for its aniseed confections and stunning monastery.

3. * **Vézelay:** This hilltop community is renowned for its breathtaking views of the surrounding countryside and its majestic church.

4. Gevrey-Chambertin is well-known for its top-notch wines, particularly Chambertin.

5. Especially Meursault, this village is recognized for its world-class wines.

6. * Vosne-Romanée: This region is famed for its wines, particularly Romanée-Conti.

7. Clos Vougeot is a wine variety from this village that is well-known around the world.

8. * **Aloxe-Corton:** This community is recognized for its top-quality wines, particularly Corton.

9. * Puligny-Montrachet is renowned for its top-notch wines, particularly Montrachet.

10. * **Chassagne-Montrachet:** This town is famed for its fine wines, particularly Montrachet.

11. * **Santenay:** This hamlet, particularly Santenay, is recognized for its world-class wines.

12. * **Pommard:** This village, particularly Pommard, is recognized for its world-class wines.

These are only a few of the Côte-d'Or's enchanting towns and villages. The Côte-d'Or has plenty to offer everyone with its rich history, culture, and breathtaking scenery.

In these cities and villages, you can accomplish the following things:

-* Visit the nearby wineries and savor the top-notch wines.
-* Investigate the medieval lanes and streets.
-* Visit the cathedrals and churches in the area.
-* Visit the regional art galleries and museums.
- * Delight in the delectable local cuisine.
-* Explore the surrounding countryside on foot or by bicycle.
-* Visit the nearby markets and stores.

Whatever your hobbies is, the Côte-d'Or is sure to have something for you to enjoy.

Regions of Burgundy

7. Saône-et-Loire

The French department of Saône-et-Loire is located in the Burgundy region. It is well-known for its wine, cuisine, and stunning scenery. Several lovely towns and villages may be found in the department, including Mâcon, Chalon-sur-Saône, Autun, and Montceau-les-Mines.

7.1 Macon

The department of Saône-et-Loire is headquartered in Mâcon. It is a city with a storied past and vibrant present. The Musée des Ursulines, La Maison de Bois, Église Saint-Pierre, Hôtel de Ville, Tour Philippe le Bon, and Porte Guillaume are just a few of the city's noteworthy historical landmarks.

Mâcon is renowned for its wine as well. The city is home to several well-known wineries and is situated in the heart of the Burgundy wine region. Visitors to Mâcon can partake in wine tastings at the nearby wineries or buy wine to bring home.

Mâcon is renowned for its cuisine in addition to its wine. Numerous top-notch eateries in the city provide both classic Burgundian fare and more contemporary, inventive cuisine.

7.1.1 City Highlights

The French city of Mâcon is located in the Burgundy region. It is renowned for its culinary, wine, and stunning old town.

1. The **Musée des Ursulines**, which is housed in a former Ursuline convent, contains a collection of artwork and historical items.

2. * **La Maison de Bois:** One of Mâcon's oldest structures, this half-timbered home is also home to a historical museum.

3. One of the most significant places of worship in Mâcon is the Romanesque Église Saint-Pierre.

4. * **Hôtel de Ville:** This town hall is a stunning Renaissance structure.

5. The Tour Philippe le Bon provides breathtaking views of Mâcon and is a relic of medieval city fortifications.

6. * **Porte Guillaume:** One of Mâcon's most recognizable monuments, this gate is another reminder of the medieval city fortifications.

7. The botanical garden at Mâcon is home to a wide range of plants from around the globe.

8. * **Parc de la Colombière:** Both locals and visitors frequent this park to unwind and take in the fresh air.

9. * **Parc de la Toison d'Or:** This park has a zoo, a playground, and a lake among its many attractions.

7.1.2 Activities Outside

You can engage in the following outdoor activities in Mâcon:

1.* **Hiking and biking:** The region around Mâcon has several hiking and biking paths that provide breathtaking views of the surrounding countryside and vineyards. The GR76 and the GR7 are two well-liked hiking routes. The Véloroute des Grands Vins and the Voie Bleue are two well-known bike routes.

2. * **Kayaking and canoeing:** Numerous businesses provide kayak and canoe rentals, and the Saône River passes through Mâcon. To reach the neighboring communities of Charnay-lès-Mâcon and Saint-Martin-Belle-Roche, you can kayak or paddle downstream.

3. The Saône River is a well-liked location for fishing. You may go pike, perch, and carp fishing.

4. The Golf de Mâcon-La Salle and the Golf de Mâcon-Charnay are just two of the golf courses in the vicinity of Mâcon.

5. several stables in the region provide horseback riding tours. You can either take a lesson or ride through the countryside and wineries.

7.2 The Abbey and History of Cluny

France's Burgundy region includes the little town of Cluny in the Saône-et-Loire region. One of the most significant religious hubs in Europe throughout the Middle Ages was the old Benedictine abbey, Cluny Abbey.

7.2.1 Cluny Abbey

In the year 910, William I, Duke of Aquitaine, founded Cluny Abbey. William gave the land for the abbey's construction, and it was immune from secular law. As a result of having this freedom to follow its own rules and regulations, the abbey swiftly rose to prominence among other Benedictine monasteries in Europe.

The 11th century saw the height of Cluny Abbey's influence. It possessed around 3,000 monasteries across Europe at the time. Another significant hub of learning and culture was Cluny Abbey. It possessed a vast library, and the monks there were renowned intellectuals.

The French Revolution substantially devastated Cluny Abbey. Its remains, however, are nonetheless striking and provide a glimpse of its previous splendor. The abbey church, which at the time of its construction was the biggest church in the world, is now a museum.

7.2.2 Medieval Buildings and Cultural Heritage

There are many additional medieval buildings and heritage sites in Cluny in addition to the Abbaye de Cluny. These consist of:

1. The Hôtel de Ville, a Renaissance-style town hall with a stunning exterior. It was constructed in the sixteenth century and now serves as a museum.

2. The Tour Philippe le Bon provides breathtaking views of Cluny and is a relic of the ancient city fortifications. It bears the name of Philip the Good, Duke of Burgundy, and was constructed in the 15th century.

3. * **The Porte Guillaume:** One of Cluny's most recognizable monuments, this gate is another piece of the ancient city walls. It bears the name William IV, Duke of Burgundy, and was constructed in the 15th century.

4. * **The Musée d'Art et d'Histoire:** This institution is home to a collection of artwork and historical relics, including paintings, sculptures, and pieces of furniture.

5. A collection of costumes from the 18th to the 20th century can be found in the Musée du Costume.

Beautiful and historically significant, Cluny is a town. The Abbaye de Cluny remains can be explored by visitors, who can also see the Hôtel de Ville, the Tour Philippe le Bon, and the Porte Guillaume. The Musée d'Art et d'Histoire and the Musée du Costume provide information on Cluny's past.

7.2.3 Cluny Today

A lot of people travel to Cluny. The Musée d'Art et d'Histoire and the Musée du Costume both offer historical information on Cluny, and visitors can also explore the abbey's remains and the town's medieval buildings.

Wine is another specialty of Cluny. There are numerous vineyards around that provide tours and tastings, and the town is situated right in the middle of the Mâconnais wine region.

Beautiful and historically significant, Cluny is a town. For everyone interested in medieval history and culture, it is a must-visit location.

7.3 Autun

France's Burgundy area includes the town of Autun. It is renowned for its stunning ancient town, natural attractions, and Roman architecture.

7.3.1 Roman Architecture

Numerous well-preserved Roman structures can be seen in Autun, which was a significant Roman city. These consist of:

1. * "Temple of Janus": One of France's best-preserved Roman temples, this structure dates to the first century AD.

2. One of the four remaining gates from the Roman city walls is the Porte d'Arroux. Its 2nd-century AD construction is adorned with reliefs showing Roman gods and goddesses.

3. One of the four remaining gates from the Roman city walls is the Porte Saint-André. It was constructed in the

second century AD and has Roman soldier reliefs all over it.

4. The Roman Theater of Atun was constructed in the first century AD and had a capacity of 15,000 spectators. Today shows and concerts take place there.

5. The Roman city walls of Atun were constructed in the second century AD and are still mostly intact. Visitors can stroll along the walls and take in breathtaking town views.

7.3.2 Natural Wonders

Autun is situated in a stunning natural environment. Hills, woods, and meadows are all around the town. In the vicinity of Autun, there are several natural wonders, such as:

1. Morvan Regional Natural Park: This area of land, which lies immediately north of Autun, is home to a variety of animals, including deer, wild boar, and eagles.

There are numerous hiking paths and waterfalls in the park.

2. * **Lac de Saint-Point:** This lake, about 20 kilometers from Autun, is a well-liked location for boating, swimming, and fishing.

3. One of the tallest waterfalls in France is the Cascade du Hérisson, which is roughly 30 miles from Autun.

7.4 Additional Villages and Towns

Saône-et-Loire is home to a number of lovely towns and villages in addition to the cities and towns of Mâcon, Cluny, and Autun. Here is a quick rundown of some of the most well-known:

1. Semur-en-Brionnais is a hilltop town renowned for its exquisite architecture and well-preserved medieval defenses. The town's winding streets and lanes are open for exploration, as are the Romanesque church and the breathtaking views of the surrounding landscape.

2. Flavigny-sur-Ozerain is a charming hamlet well-known for its aniseed confections and stunning monastery. Visitors can meander around the picturesque village square, visit the abbey church, and take a tour of the anise factory.

3. * **Vézelay:** This hilltop community is renowned for its breathtaking views of the surrounding countryside and its majestic church. The basilica is one of France's most significant Romanesque churches and a UNESCO World Heritage Site.

4. Gevrey-Chambertin is well-known for its top-notch wines, particularly Chambertin. The best wines in the world are available for tasting, wine excursions, and vineyard visits.

5. Especially Meursault, this village is recognized for its world-class wines. The best wines in the world are available for tasting, wine excursions, and vineyard visits.

6. * Vosne-Romanée: This region is famed for its wines, particularly Romanée-Conti. The best wines in the world are available for tasting, wine excursions, and vineyard visits.

7. Clos Vougeot is a wine variety from this village that is well-known around the world. The best wines in the world are available for tasting, wine excursions, and vineyard visits.

8. * **Aloxe-Corton:** This community is recognized for its top-quality wines, particularly Corton. The best wines in the world are available for tasting, wine excursions, and vineyard visits.

9. * Puligny-Montrachet is renowned for its top-notch wines, particularly Montrachet. The best wines in the world are available for tasting, wine excursions, and vineyard visits.

10. * **Chassagne-Montrachet:** This town is famed for its fine wines, particularly Montrachet. The best

wines in the world are available for tasting, wine excursions, and vineyard visits.

11. * **Santenay:** This hamlet, particularly Santenay, is recognized for its world-class wines. The best wines in the world are available for tasting, wine excursions, and vineyard visits.

12. * **Pommard:** This village, particularly Pommard, is recognized for its world-class wines. The best wines in the world are available for tasting, wine excursions, and vineyard visits.

Saône-et-Loire is also home to a variety of other attractive villages in addition to these wine villages. Here are some of the most well-liked:

1. *Tournus: This community is renowned for its lovely Romanesque abbey and charming town square. Visitors can wander through the village square, visit the abbey church, and savor the mouthwatering regional food.

2. The well-preserved medieval walls and breathtaking vistas of the surrounding countryside are two of this walled village's most well-known features. In addition to visiting the castle ruins and taking in the panoramic views, visitors can explore the village's winding streets and lanes.

3. * **La Clayette:** This market town is renowned for both its bustling outdoor market and its attractive town square. Visitors can browse the market stalls, go to the neighborhood stores, and savor the delectable local fare.

4. * Marcigny: This community is renowned for its charming riverbank and lovely half-timbered homes. The town's historic district may be explored on foot, local eateries and stores can be visited, and the tranquil riverfront backdrop can be enjoyed.

5. *Paray-le-Monial: This community is renowned for its stunning basilica and its extensive religious history. Visitors can explore the Basilica church, go to the nearby

cafes and stores, and take in the tranquility of this quaint town.

These are only a few of the Saône-et-Loire's quaint towns and villages. Everybody may find something to enjoy in Saône-et-Loire thanks to its rich history, culture, and natural beauty.

Regions of Burgundy

8. Yonne

The French department of Yonne is located in the Burgundy-Franche-Comté region. The Yonne River, which runs through the department, inspired its naming. The Yonne is renowned for its stunning scenery, extensive history, and mouthwatering cuisine.

8.1. Auxerre

Auxerre is a city in the Burgundy-Franche-Comté region of north-central France's Yonne department. It serves as the Yonne department's capital.

8.1.1 "Historic Attractions"

Auxerre has a lengthy history that dates back to the Roman era. During the Middle Ages, the city was a significant hub of study and culture. There are several historical sites in Auxerre, including:

1. The Gothic cathedral in Auxerre is one of the most significant places of worship in the Yonne. A multitude of stained glass windows and sculptures can be seen in the cathedral, which dates back to the 13th and 14th centuries.

2. One of the earliest places of worship in the Yonne is the Benedictine abbey of Saint-Germain, founded in the sixth century. The Romanesque abbey church features a stunning Gothic choir.

3. The former Abbey of Saint-Germain now serves as home to the Musée de l'Abbaye Saint-Germain, which features a collection of artwork and artifacts from the abbey's past. The museum also features a garden where guests can unwind and take in the fresh air.

4. * **Musée Leblanc-Duvernoy:** This museum is housed in a mansion from the 16th century and has a collection of works of art and historical objects from the Yonne. The museum also features a garden where guests can unwind and take in the fresh air.

5. * **Tour de l'Horloge:** One of Auxerre's most recognizable landmarks is this clock tower. A clock from the 14th century is housed in the tower, which was constructed in the 15th century.

8.1.2 *Cultural Celebrations*

Throughout the year, Auxerre is the site of numerous cultural gatherings. The most well-liked occasions include:

1. International Festival of Classical Music in Auxerre: This event is held annually in July and offers a range of events, including concerts, recitals, and masterclasses.

2. * **Festival International de Folklore d'Auxerre:** This folklore gathering takes place in August and includes a range of performances, including singing, dancing, and instrumental music.

3. * **Festival International de Théâtre d'Auxerre:** This theater event takes place in September and presents

a range of performances, including plays, musicals, and dance.

4. * **Festival International de Danse d'Auxerre:** This dance event is held annually in October and showcases a range of performances, including ballet, modern dance, and traditional dance.

5. * **Festival International de Cinéma d'Auxerre:** This film festival presents a selection of movies from all around the world each year in November.

8.2 Vézelay - Spirituality and Pilgrimage

A hilltop village in France's Burgundy-Franche-Comté region called Vézelay may be found in the Yonne department. It is a significant hub for pilgrimage and a UNESCO World Heritage Site.

8.2.1 Vezélay Abbey

In the ninth century, the Benedictine Abbey of Vézelay was established. During the Middle Ages, the abbey was a significant hub of study and culture. It was also a significant pilgrimage site, drawing travelers from all around Europe.

The Romanesque abbey church was erected in the 12th and 13th centuries. Numerous sculptures and stained glass windows can be found inside the church. Visitors can view Saint Mary Magdalene's relics in the abbey's crypt.

8.2.2 Baselique Sainte-Marie-Madeleine

The Romanesque Basilique Sainte-Marie-Madeleine was erected in the 12th and 13th centuries. Numerous sculptures and stained glass windows can be found inside the church. Visitors can view Saint Mary Magdalene's relics in the church's crypt.

8.2.3 Routes of Pilgrimage and Spiritual Journeys

Vézelay is accessible by a variety of different pilgrimage routes. The Via Lemovicensis, which originates in Limoges and ends in Vézelay, is one of the most well-known routes. The 480-kilometer Via Lemovicensis travels through some of France's most stunning landscapes.

The Via Francigena, which begins in Canterbury and finishes in Rome, is another well-traveled pilgrimage path to Vézelay. The 2,000-kilometer Via Francigena travels through France, Switzerland, Italy, and the Vatican City.

Additionally, pilgrims have the option of designing their own personal route to Vézelay. Books, websites, and apps are just a few of the options available to aid pilgrims in planning their itinerary.

8.2.4 Local customs and pilgrimage occasions

In Vézelay, there are numerous regional customs and pilgrimage occasions. The visit to the crypt of the abbey church is among the most well-liked customs. To pray to Saint Mary Magdalene and to see her relics, pilgrims visit the crypt.

The Feast of Saint Mary Magdalene, which takes place on July 22, is an additional well-liked pilgrimage occasion. In Vézelay, the Feast of Saint Mary Magdalene is a significant religious celebration that draws visitors from all over the world.

There are several other pilgrimage occasions celebrated in Vézelay throughout the year, in addition to the pilgrimage to the crypt of the abbey church and the Feast of Saint Mary Magdalene. These things happen, like:

1. The Holy Week Pilgrimage: This journey takes place during the week before Easter, during Holy Week. The

activities that pilgrims partake in include Mass, processions, and meditation.

2. * The Assumption Pilgrimage: This pilgrimage takes place on August 15, which is the feast day of the Virgin Mary's Assumption. The activities that pilgrims partake in include Mass, processions, and meditation.

3. * The All Saints' Day Pilgrimage: This journey takes place on November 1, which is All Saints' Day. The activities that pilgrims partake in include Mass, processions, and meditation.

These are only a few of the numerous pilgrimage occasions that take place in Vézelay all year long. There is constantly something going on for pilgrims of all faiths in the thriving pilgrimage site of Vézelay.

<u>**Tips for Arranging a Vézelay Pilgrimage**</u>

Here are some suggestions for organizing a visit to Vézelay:

-* Decide on the ideal pilgrimage path for you. To get to Vézelay, there are a variety of pilgrimage paths, each with its own special difficulties and rewards.

-* Arrange your pilgrimage ahead of time. This involves reserving lodging, travel, and pilgrimage tickets.

-* Be sure to prepare for any weather. It's crucial to be ready for everything because the weather in Vézelay is prone to sudden changes.

– Be receptive to novel experiences. A journey, both physically and spiritually, is what pilgrimage is. Be willing to discover new things about the world and about yourself.

Whatever your reason for traveling to Vézelay, it will undoubtedly be a fulfilling and memorable experience.

8.3 Chablis

A little town called Chablis may be found in the Yonne department of north-central France's Burgundy-Franche-Comté region. It serves as the Chablis wine region's capital. The Chardonnay grape is used to produce the dry white wines that are so popular in Chablis.

8.3.1 Vineyards and Wine Tasting

In Chablis, many wineries provide tours and wine tastings. Visitors can sample various Chablis wines while learning about the wine-making process.

In Chablis, some of the most well-known wineries are:

(1) Domaine Laroche
2. Domaine William Fèvre domain
3. Domaine Drouhin-Vaudon
4. Domaine Raveneau

5. Domaine Jean-Marc Brocard

Visitors can stroll among the vineyards in Chablis in addition to visiting wineries. The hillsides surrounding the town of Chablis are home to the Chablis vineyards. Visitors can take in the stunning surroundings while learning about the various soil and climate types that contribute to the distinctive characteristics of Chablis wines.

8.3.2 Local Food

Chablis is renowned for its delectable regional food as well. In Chablis, some of the most well-liked dishes are:

1. Escargots are sautéed snails with butter and garlic.
2. Coq au vin is chicken that has been cooked with bacon, mushrooms, and red wine.
3. * Beef bourguignon: Beef cooked with red wine, onions, and mushrooms.
4. A soft cow's milk cheese produced in the Chablis region is known as "Chablis cheese."

5. A custard dessert with a crust made of caramelized sugar is known as crème brûlée.

One of the many restaurants in Chablis offers visitors the chance to sample the regional cuisine. Among the most well-known eateries are:

1. Le Bistrot des Grands Hommes
2. Le Close Des Hospice
3. La Côte Saint-Jacques
4. La Table du Gourmet
5. Le Relais du Vieux Chablis"

8.4 Additional Cities and Towns

Here are some further Yonne department towns and villages worth visiting:

1. Sens: Sens, the second-largest city in the Yonne department, is renowned for its Gothic cathedral, which dates back to the 12th and 13th centuries and is one of the oldest in Europe. Numerous sculptures and stained

glass windows can be found inside the cathedral. The Musée de Sens, which exhibits a collection of artwork and historical objects, is another attraction in Sens.

2. * **Joigny:** The Yonne River runs through the lovely town of Joigny. The town is renowned for its bustling market and half-timbered homes. The Musée de Joigny, which exhibits a variety of artwork and relics from the town's past, is another attraction in Joigny.

3. Avallon is a charming town located in the Morvan highlands. The town is well-known for both its picturesque surroundings and its ancient castle. The Musée d'Avallon, which exhibits a collection of artwork and relics from the town's past, is also located in Avallon.

4. Tonnerre is a historic settlement on the Armançon River. The town's stunning cathedral and half-timbered homes are well-known attractions. The Musée du Tonnerrois, which exhibits a collection of artwork and relics from the town's past, is also located in Tonnerre.

5. * **Noyers:** In the Serain valley, there is a beautiful village called Noyers. The hamlet is renowned for its magnificent homes and its ancient walls. The Musée de Noyers, which exhibits a collection of artwork and relics from the village's past, is another attraction in Noyers.

6. * **Vézelay:** Vézelay is a significant site for pilgrimage and a UNESCO World Heritage Site. The town is renowned for its stunning countryside and Romanesque abbey church. The Musée de Vézelay, which exhibits a variety of artwork and relics from the town's past, is another attraction in Vézelay.

These are only a small sample of the several towns and villages in the Yonne region that are worthwhile seeing. There is something for everyone in the lovely Yonne, which has a rich history and culture.

9. Transportation And Costs

9.1 How to Travel to Burgundy

Depending on where you're coming from, there are various routes to reach Burgundy.

1. Via plane

Dijon Airport (DIJ), which is situated around 6 kilometers from the city of Dijon, is the nearest airport to Burgundy. But because Dijon Airport is a very tiny airport, there aren't many direct flights from other significant cities.

Flying into Paris Charles de Gaulle Airport (CDG) or Paris Orly Airport (ORY) is a preferable choice. There are numerous direct flights to both of these airports from other significant global cities. You can go to Burgundy by train or bus from Paris.

2. By train:

The fastest way to go by train to Burgundy is with the TGV high-speed train. From Paris to Dijon, there are direct TGV trains that take about one hour and forty minutes. Regional trains go from Dijon to Burgundy's other towns and villages.

From other significant French towns like Lyon and Marseille, you can easily catch a train to Burgundy. The trip will take longer than if you take a TGV from Paris, though.

3. By bus:
In Burgundy, there are numerous bus companies in operation. Buses can carry you to tiny settlements that the train network doesn't reach even if they are slower than trains and cost less money.

You can check out the websites of the following businesses to learn more about bus routes that go through Burgundy:

Mobigo -

Flixbus -
Ouibus

4. By car:

It is advised to rent a car if you intend to explore smaller villages or wineries. You'll be free to take your time and discover the area at your own speed as a result.

In Burgundy, several automobile rental agencies are active. The airport and various Dijon locales also offer automobile rentals.

<u>**Below are some suggestions for traveling to Burgundy:**</u>

-* If you're flying into Paris, get your rail or bus tickets in advance, especially if you're going during a busy time of year.

-* If you're on a tight budget, think about using the bus. Buses can be slower and less convenient than trains, but keep that in mind.

-* It is advised to rent a car if you intend to visit smaller villages or wineries.

-* If you're driving, make sure you get a vignette. In France, vignettes are necessary for driving on the highways.

9.2 Buses and Trains for Public Transportation

The central French region of Burgundy is renowned for its picturesque countryside, mouthwatering cuisine, fine wines, and charming towns and villages. By train, bus, and car, the region is well-connected to the rest of France and Europe.

1.**Trains**

The train is the most effective mode of public transportation for getting around Burgundy. The major towns and villages in the area are connected by a good network of train lines. The trains provide a picturesque way to travel across the countryside and are comfortable and dependable.

You can take a TGV high-speed train from Paris to Dijon, the capital of Burgundy, to get there by train. The trip lasts approximately 1 hour and 40 minutes. Regional trains go from Dijon to Burgundy's other towns and villages.

Online or at the train station, you can purchase train tickets. It is recommended to purchase your tickets in advance if you intend to travel during a busy period.

2. **Buses**

In Burgundy, numerous bus companies run their operations. Buses can carry you to tiny settlements that the train network doesn't reach even if they are slower than trains and cost less money.

9.3 Driving Advice and Car Rentals

The lovely Burgundy area in central France is distinguished by its rolling hills, vineyards, and charming villages. Driving is among the greatest ways to discover Burgundy. This provides you the freedom to travel to more remote wineries and smaller communities that aren't served by the public transportation system.

Automobile rentals

In Burgundy, several automobile rental agencies are active. The airport and several places in Dijon, Burgundy's capital, both offer automobile rentals.

Make careful to compare rates from various companies before booking a rental car in Burgundy. To fully comprehend the terms and conditions, you should carefully read the rental agreement.

Driving Advice

Burgundy is a typically safe and simple place to drive. There are several considerations you should make, though:

1. The maximum allowed speed on highways is 130 km/h. In cities and villages, the posted speed limit is 50 km/h.

2. * Watch out for pedestrians and bikers. In crosswalks, they have the right of way.

3. * Be prepared for winding, narrow roads.

4. * Be cautious when parking, especially in cities and villages. Parking spots may be scarce.

9.4 Routes for Bicycling and Riding

Getting around Burgundy's picturesque countryside and quaint villages on a bicycle is a terrific idea. In the area, numerous well-maintained bicycle routes range in difficulty.

Here are some of Burgundy's most well-known bike routes:

1. The 212-kilometer-long "Burgundian Canal Cycle Route" follows the Burgundy Canal, which links the Yonne and Saône rivers. Cycling enthusiasts of all skill levels will find the route to be a suitable choice as it is largely flat and well-signposted.

2. From Nevers to Saint-Nazaire, 610 kilometers of the Loire à Vélo cycle path follow the river. The Loire Valley, a UNESCO World Heritage Site, and other parts of France's most breathtaking countryside are also traversed on this trip.

3. The Morvan Cycle Route is a 340-kilometer route that passes through the southern Burgundy mountains known as the Morvans. The path has spectacular vistas of the Morvan countryside but is more difficult than the other routes on our list.

In addition to these significant bike routes, Burgundy has a variety of lesser riding routes.

The following organizations' websites have information about these routes:

1. Velo Bourgogne-Franche-Comté.
2. French Velo Tourisme
3. Tourism in Bourgogne

The following advice should be taken into account as you prepare to bicycle across Burgundy:

-* Pick a bike route that is suitable for your experience and level of fitness.

-* Don't forget to bring the required equipment, such as a helmet, a water bottle, and a repair kit.

-* Be mindful of the weather and dress appropriately.

-* On lengthy trips, stop sometimes. Along the bike routes, there are a lot of cafes and eateries.

-* Take in the view! Cycling around Burgundy is a fantastic way to see the area.

9.5 Options for Ride-sharing and Taxi Services

Although there aren't many ride-sharing and taxi choices in Burgundy, there are few.

Services for taxis

In Burgundy, there are numerous taxi firms in operation. In all of the region's major towns and cities, taxi services are available.

You can use a taxi app like G7 or MyTaxi to book a ride, or you can call the taxi company directly.

In Burgundy, taxi fares are subject to government regulation. The prices are determined by the route taken and the time of day.

Ride-Sharing Alternatives

There are currently no ride-sharing services like Uber and Lyft in Burgundy. However, a few French ride-sharing businesses, including LeCab and BlaBlaCar, are present in the area.

On the long-distance ride-sharing website BlaBlaCar, drivers can offer seats in their vehicles to those heading in the same direction. Users of the taxi app LeCab can reserve cabs and ride-hailing services.

You must download the app and register for an account with a ride-sharing service before you can use it. You may look for rides and reserve a seat after creating an account.

9.6 Travel Expenses and Cheap Travel Advice

The lovely Burgundy area in central France is distinguished by its rolling hills, vineyards, and charming villages. Additionally, traveling there is not cheap. But there are other methods to cut costs when visiting Burgundy.

1.**Accommodation**

When visiting Burgundy, one of the largest expenses is lodging. The majority of hotels in the area have expensive rates. Hostels, guesthouses, and Airbnbs are just a few of the various options for inexpensive lodging.

Here are some suggestions for locating inexpensive lodging in Burgundy:

-* Reserve your lodging in advance, especially if you are traveling during a popular time of year.

-* Take into account staying in a smaller town or village away from the main tourist destinations.

-* Seek out lodging that provides discounts for extended stays.

-* Think about reserving a room at a hostel or inn.

-* Renting affordable homes and flats is easy with Airbnb.

2. **Food**

Another significant cost when visiting Burgundy is food. The cost of eating out can be high in this area. However, there are several ways to reduce the cost of your food, including making your own food at home and taking advantage of happy hour discounts.

The following advice will help you spend less on food in Burgundy:

-* Eat at neighborhood cafes and bistros. Usually, they provide meals at lower prices than restaurants.

-* Prepare your own food. This is a fantastic method to cut costs, especially if you are staying at an Airbnb or another type of self-catering facility.

-* Benefit from happy hour discounts. In Burgundy, a lot of taverns and eateries offer drink and food specials during happy hour.

-* Explore regional markets. At neighborhood markets, you can purchase fresh foods at a fraction of the cost of what you would pay at a supermarket.

3. **Transportation**

Traveling to Burgundy can also be expensive in terms of transportation. A car is the most practical means of transportation in the area. However, the cost of renting an automobile can be expensive. If you're on a tight budget, think about taking the bus or renting a bike.

Here are some recommendations for reducing transportation costs in Burgundy:

-* Take the bus or train. Using trains and buses to go about Burgundy is rather inexpensive.

-* Get a bike to rent. This is an excellent method to save money on transportation while independently exploring the area.

-* Think about getting a regional pass. If you want to travel a lot by public transit, think about getting a regional pass. Long-term, this will save you money on fares.

4. **Activities**

In Burgundy, there are plenty of free and inexpensive things to do. The most well-liked free activities are biking, hiking, and visiting nearby cathedrals and churches.

Here are some recommendations for budget-friendly activities in Burgundy:

-* Make use of free activities like biking, hiking, and visiting nearby cathedrals and churches.

- * Keep an eye out for activity discounts. Student, elder, and group discounts are frequently available at museums and other attractions.

-* Think about getting a pass. Several attractions provide passes that grant you cheap access to several attractions.

Budget Advice

Here are some other suggestions for visiting Burgundy on a tight budget:

-* Before your trip, make a budget and follow it.

-* Keep tabs on your spending while you're away.

-* Avoid making impulsive purchases.

-* Take breaks from sightseeing to avoid spending too much money on refreshments.

-* To avoid paying excessive fees during peak season, travel between April and May and September and October.

These recommendations can help you travel to Burgundy on a budget while still having a fantastic experience.

10. Accommodation And Prices

10.1 Accommodation Styles

Burgundy offers a wide range of lodging choices, from high-end hotels to affordable hostels. Your budget, travel interests, and style will all influence the kind of lodging you select.

The following are some of the most well-liked lodging options in Burgundy:

1. Hotels: In Burgundy, hotels are the most popular kind of lodging. From chain hotels that are affordable to luxurious boutique hotels, there are accommodations for every budget.

2. Hostels: Hostels are an excellent choice for tourists on a tight budget. Dorm beds and private rooms are also available in hostels, and many have common kitchens and dining spaces where visitors can prepare their own meals.

3. Guesthouses: For tourists seeking a more personalized experience, guesthouses are a good choice. In contrast to hotels, guesthouses are often owned by families and provide a more personal experience.

4. Airbnbs: For travelers looking for a distinctive and reasonably priced place to stay, Airbnbs are a popular choice. From apartments and homes to renovated barns and farmhouses, Airbnbs come in all sizes and kinds.

5. Self-catering cottages are a good choice for families and groups of people. Typically situated in rural locations, self-catering cottages include a fully furnished kitchen where visitors can prepare their own meals.

6. Campgrounds: Budget travelers and outdoor enthusiasts frequently choose to camp. Burgundy is home to several campgrounds, from modest ones with few amenities to opulent ones with swimming pools and other entertainment options.

The following elements should be taken into account when selecting lodging in Burgundy:

1. Budget: Depending on the type of lodging, the region, and the season, lodging expenses change.

2. Travel style: Do you like a more opulent experience or are you a budget traveler seeking for a simple place to stay?

3. Preferences: Would you rather live in a city or out in the country? Do you want to live near popular tourist destinations or away from the crowds?

After giving these things some thought, you can begin to limit your options. Before making a reservation, be careful to check reviews of various lodging alternatives to have a better understanding of what to anticipate.

10.2 Resorts and Hotels

Burgundy offers a selection of lodging options, from chain hotels that are affordable to opulent five-star resorts.

Some of the most well-known lodgings in Burgundy are listed below:

1. Hotel Le Cep: This five-star establishment is situated in Beaune, Burgundy's winemaking center. Luxurious lodgings, a Michelin-starred restaurant, and a top-notch wine cellar are all provided at Hotel Le Cep.

2. The four-star Château de Vault de Lugny hotel is situated in the Burgundy region. There are luxurious lodgings, a fine-dining restaurant, and a spa at Château de Vault de Lugny.

3. The charming village of Levernois is home to the four-star Hostellerie de Levernois. Hostellerie de Levernois provides enticing lodgings, a restaurant with a Michelin star, and a swimming pool.

4. Château Sainte Sabine: Situated in the Sainte Sabine village, this three-star chateau hotel. A restaurant, a swimming pool, and nice lodgings are available at Château Sainte Sabine.

5. The three-star L'Hôtel de Beaune is situated in the heart of Beaune. There are contemporary lodgings, a bistro, and a cafe at L'Hôtel de Beaune.

6. The four-star Domaine de Rymska - Relais & Châteaux hotel is situated in the Burgundy countryside. The restaurant, pool, and rustic-chic lodgings at Domaine de Rymska - Relais & Châteaux are available.

10.3 Bed and (B&Bs)

Bed and breakfasts (B&Bs) are a type of lodging that provides both a place to stay overnight and breakfast. B&Bs offer a more individualized experience and are often smaller than hotels.

Travelers who are looking for a distinctive and reasonably priced location to stay might consider B&Bs. B&Bs are frequently found in picturesque locations, such as historic structures, rural communities, or coastal towns.

Some of the most well-known B&Bs in Burgundy are listed below:

1. Le Clos de la Violette: This B&B is situated in the center of Dijon, Burgundy's city. Le Clos de la Violette provides cozy lodgings, a sumptuous breakfast, and a convenient location.

2. La Maison d'Hôtes de Charme is a bed and breakfast situated in the charming town of Beaune. The La Maison d'Hôtes de Charme offers opulent lodgings, a delectable breakfast, and a terrace with village views.

3. The B&B known as "Le Relais de la Poste" is situated in the historic village of Vézelay. The lovely lodgings, filling breakfast, and breathtaking views of the countryside are all provided by Le Relais de la Poste.

The following are some benefits of staying at a B&B:

-* **B&Bs are often owned by families and provide a more individualized experience than hotels. The owners of B&Bs are frequently delighted to make suggestions for places to go and activities to do nearby.

-* **Unique accommodations:** B&Bs provide a range of unusual lodging options, including renovated barns and farmhouses as well as historic homes.

-* **Affordable costs:** B&Bs are frequently less expensive than hotels.

-* **Delicious breakfasts:** B&Bs are renowned for their sumptuous breakfasts, which are frequently prepared with fresh, regional ingredients.

10.4 Holiday Homes and Vacation Rentals

For tourists searching for a more roomy and economical location to stay, vacation rentals and holiday homes are a terrific choice. From flats and homes to converted barns and farmhouses, vacation rentals and holiday homes come in various sizes and styles.

Families, parties, and tourists who plan to stay in Burgundy for a long time should choose vacation rentals and holiday homes. Kitchens are frequently available in vacation rentals and holiday houses, which helps save food expenses.

Here are a few of the most well-liked holiday houses and rental properties in Burgundy:

1. La Maison de la Colline is a holiday home right in the middle of Beaune. A large four-bedroom property with a fully functional kitchen, a private garden, and a terrace is available at La Maison de la Colline.

2. Le Gîte du Vigneron: This holiday home is situated in the Burgundy countryside. A beautiful two-bedroom cottage with a fully functional kitchen, a private garden, and a grill is available at Le Gîte du Vigneron.

3. Le Moulin de la Rivière is a holiday rental in the Burgundy countryside that is situated on a river. Unique

three-bedroom converted windmill, Le Moulin de la Rivière, features a fully functional kitchen, a private garden, and a terrace with river views.

10.5 Outdoor lodging and Camping

A wonderful way to appreciate the great outdoors and take in Burgundy's natural beauty is to go camping. Burgundy offers a wide range of camping options, from budget campgrounds with basic amenities to upscale campgrounds with pools and other recreational activities.

Here are some of Burgundy's most well-liked camping and outdoor lodging options:

1. *Camping Huttopia Meursault: This campground is situated right in the middle of Burgundy's wine country. There are several different types of lodging available at Camping Huttopia Meursault, including tent pitches, cabins, and glamping tents. The campground also features a restaurant, a bar, and a swimming pool.

2. * Campsite & Bistrot de Messeugne: This restaurant is situated in the Burgundy countryside. A range of lodging options are available at Camping & Bistrot de Messeugne, including tent sites, trailers, and mobile homes. The campground also features a restaurant, a bar, and a swimming pool.

3. The village of Chagny is home to the campground known as Paquier Fane. Tent pitches, travel trailers, and mobile homes are just a few of the lodging options available at Camping Paquier Fane. The campground also features a restaurant, a bar, and a swimming pool.

4. In the town of Saint-Honoré-les-Bains, there is a campground called Camping et Gites des Bains. Tent pitches, travel trailers, and mobile homes are just a few of the lodging options available at Camping et Gites des Bains. The campground also features a restaurant, a bar, and a swimming pool.

5. On the Saône River's banks is a campground called "Camping de la Rivière." A range of lodging options are

available at Camping de la Rivière, including tent sites, trailers, and mobile homes. The campground also features a restaurant, a bar, and a swimming pool.

10.6 Lodging Prices and Booking Advice

The price of lodging in Burgundy varies according to the kind of lodging, the area, and the season. Here is a general breakdown of lodging expenses in Burgundy:

1.* **Hotels:** A budget hotel in Burgundy can cost as little as €50 per night, while a five-star hotel can cost as much as €300 per night.

2. * **Hostels:** In Burgundy, a dorm bed costs about €20 per night, while a private room costs about €50.

3. * **Guesthouses:** In Burgundy, rates for guesthouses range from about €70 for a basic room to €150 for a deluxe room.

4. The size and location of the house affect the pricing of an Airbnb in Burgundy. However, hotel rates are typically higher than those on Airbnb.

5. Self-catering cottage costs in Burgundy range from approximately €100 per night for a modest cottage to €300 per night for a luxury cottage.

6. * **Campgrounds:** In Burgundy, the cost of renting a mobile home at a campground ranges from about €10 per night for a tent site to €50 per night.

Here are some recommendations for lodging in Burgundy:

-* Reserve your lodging in advance, especially if you are traveling during a popular time of year.

-* Take into account staying in a smaller town or village away from the main tourist destinations. The cost of lodging is frequently lower in smaller towns and villages.

-* Seek out lodging that provides discounts for extended stays.

– Be open to changing your plans. You will probably find better prices on lodging if you can travel during the off-season or shoulder season.

-* Before making a reservation, compare prices across several websites and lodging establishments.

-* Before making a reservation, read reviews of various lodging options to get a better understanding of what to anticipate.

11. Outdoor Recreation

11.1 Discovering Burgundy's Natural Beauty

The lovely Burgundy area in central France is distinguished by its rolling hills, vineyards, and charming villages. The outdoors can be enjoyed there as well. Burgundy offers a wide range of outdoor pursuits, including hiking, riding, kayaking, canoeing, and fishing.

Here are some suggestions for discovering Burgundy's breathtaking scenery:

1.* **Hiking:** There are various hiking paths in Burgundy, ranging from straightforward strolls to strenuous hikes. The Tour du Mont Beuvray, which provides breathtaking views of the Morvan Mountains, and the GR7 (Grande Randonnée 7), which traverses the heart of Burgundy, are two of the most well-known hiking routes.

2. * **Biking:** Burgundy is a wonderful region to tour by bicycle. There are many bike trails available, including the 150-kilometer Voie Verte de Bourgogne, which follows the Canal du Nivernais.

3. Burgundy is home to several rivers and lakes that are ideal for kayaking and canoeing. Saône, Yonne, and Lake Vouglans are a few of the most well-liked streams for kayaking and canoeing.

4. Burgundy is an excellent area to go fishing. You may fish for trout, carp, and other fish in several rivers and lakes. Burgundy Canal is a good place to go fishing.

<u>Here are some specific locations where you can discover the natural beauty of Burgundy:</u>

1. Morvan Regional Natural Park: Located in the heart of Burgundy, the Morvan Regional Natural Park is

stunning. Rivers, lakes, and woodlands can be found in the park. In the park, you can hike, cycle, kayak, and canoe.

2. The Burgundy Waterway is a beautiful waterway that travels across Burgundy. You may either bike or walk along the canal towpath, or you can rent a boat and cruise along the canal.

3. * **Loire Valley:** The Loire Valley, which is close to Burgundy, is a UNESCO World Heritage Site. The Loire Valley is renowned for its exquisite vineyards, gardens, and castles.

4. * The Saône River is one of the principal rivers in Burgundy. The river offers boat tours, kayaking, and fishing opportunities.

5. Vineyards in the Côte d'Or area of Burgundy are well-known for their quality. You may either hike or bike through the vineyards and take in the view, or you can go on a wine tour of the area.

11.2 Trails for Hiking and Walking

With approximately 10,000 km of clearly marked hiking and walking routes, Burgundy offers something for people of all fitness levels. Among the most well-liked trails are:

1.* **GR7 (Grande Randonnée 7)**: This long-distance track winds through villages, vineyards, and woodlands as it traverses the center of Burgundy. Although it is a difficult trek, it offers beautiful views and the chance to see the best of Burgundy.

2. The Tour du Mont Beuvray includes the peak of Mont Beuvray, which provides sweeping views of the surrounding area and travels across the best parts of the Morvan Regional Natural Park. There are several settlements along the route where you can pause for food and water, and the track is clearly marked.

3. * **Voie Verte de Bourgogne**: This former railroad line has been transformed into a traffic-free greenway,

making it a wonderful location for cycling or walking. The route winds through vineyards, towns, and woodlands as it traverses the center of Burgundy.

4. * *Canal du Nivernais*: This beautiful canal meanders across Burgundy, passing through charming towns and open spaces. The towpath can be used for biking or walking, or you can rent a boat and cruise the canal.

5. The Côte d'Or is an area in Burgundy that is well-known for its vineyards. You can go on a scenic bike or hiking tour through the vineyards, or you can visit one of the many wineries for a sampling.

There are also some shorter walks and trails in Burgundy if you're searching for something simpler and shorter. You may, for instance, stroll around the Beaune hamlet, go to the Château de Clos Vougeot, or climb to the summit of the Roche de Solutré.

11.3 Routes for Bikes and Cyclists

Cycling is a terrific way to discover Burgundy. There are numerous cycling routes available, ranging from straightforward rides to strenuous climbs. In Burgundy, some of the most well-known bicycle routes are:

1. The "Voie Verte de Bourgogne" is a former railroad line that has been transformed into a peaceful greenway that is a wonderful area to ride or stroll. The route winds through vineyards, towns, and woodlands as it traverses the center of Burgundy.

2. *Canal du Nivernais: This beautiful canal meanders across Burgundy, passing through charming towns and open spaces. The towpath is suitable for cycling, and you can also rent a boat and cruise the canal.

3. Vineyards in the Côte d'Or area of Burgundy are well-known for their quality. You can either stop at one of the many wineries for a tasting or go cycling through the vineyards and take in the landscape.

4. * **EuroVelo 6:** This long-distance bicycle route travels through Burgundy as it makes its way from the Atlantic Ocean to the Black Sea. Although it is a difficult path, it offers breathtaking scenery and the chance to explore some of Burgundy's best.

5. * **Tour de Bourgogne à vélo:** This circular route travels through vineyards, villages, and forests, taking in the best of Burgundy. There are several settlements along the road where you can stop for food and drink, and the route is clearly marked.

There are some shorter bike routes in Burgundy if you're searching for something quicker and simpler. Cycling across the Parc Naturel Régional du Morvan, touring the Château de Clos Vougeot, or circumnavigating the village of Beaune are a few examples.

11.4 River and Water-related Activities

Burgundy offers a wide range of river and water-based activities, such as kayaking, canoeing, rafting, stand-up paddleboarding (SUP), swimming, fishing, and boat trips.

Here are some suggestions for river and water-based activities in Burgundy:

1. Canoeing and kayaking are popular activities in Burgundy because of the region's many rivers and lakes. Saône, Yonne, and Lake Vouglans are a few of the most well-liked streams for kayaking and canoeing.

2. * Rafting: The Arroux River and the Cure River are two rivers in Burgundy that are suited for rafting. Whitewater rapids can be thrilling to experience while rafting.

3. * Stand-up paddleboarding (SUP): SUP is a fantastic way to discover the tranquil lakes and rivers of Burgundy. In many different places in Burgundy, you can rent a SUP board.

4. * **Swimming:** There are several lakes and rivers in Burgundy that are ideal for swimming. The Saône River, Lake Settons, and Lake Vouglans are a few of the most well-liked swimming locations.

5. Burgundy is an excellent area to go fishing. You may fish for trout, carp, and other fish in several rivers and lakes. Burgundy Canal is a good place to go fishing.

6. * **Boat trips:** In Burgundy, there are numerous options for boat tours. You can go on a boat tour of the Saône River, Lake Vouglans, or the Burgundy Canal.

11.5 Wildlife Observation and Natural Areas

The lovely Burgundy area in central France is distinguished by its rolling hills, vineyards, and charming villages. An excellent site to see wildlife is there as well. In Burgundy, there are several natural preserves where you can witness a wide range of creatures, including birds, mammals, and reptiles.

The following are some of the top locations in Burgundy for spotting wildlife:

1. Morvan Regional Natural Park: Deer, wild boar, foxes, and badgers are among the animals that call this park home. The park is also home to a variety of species, such as woodpeckers, owls, and hawks.

2. * **Parc Naturel Régional du Haut-Jura:** A variety of animals, including chamois, marmots, and eagles, can be found here. The park also has a wide diversity of wildflowers.

3. * **Parc Naturel Régional de la Forêt d'Orient:** A variety of waterbirds, including ducks, geese, and swans, call this park home. In the park, you can also witness foxes, wild boars, and deer.

4. * **Parc Naturel Régional du Marais Poitevin:** A variety of waterbirds, including herons, egrets, and

ducks, call this park home. In the park, you can also witness beavers, otters, and water snakes.

5. * **Parc Naturel Régional de la Brenne:** A variety of species, including cranes, storks, and ducks, call this park home. In the park, you can also witness foxes, wild boars, and deer.

11.6 Aerial Adventures and Hot Air Balloon Rides

The lovely Burgundy area in central France is distinguished by Hot air balloon flights and other flying experiences can be had there as well. In Burgundy, a variety of businesses provide hot air balloon trips as well as other aerial adventures like paragliding and microlight flights.

Rides in hot air balloons are a fantastic way to experience Burgundy from a unique angle. You will enjoy breathtaking views of the vineyards, towns, and countryside as you glide through the air. Rides in hot air balloons normally last for one hour.

A fantastic method to enjoy the rush of flight is through paragliding. You will enjoy breathtaking views of the Burgundy countryside as you soar into the air. A normal paragliding flight lasts for roughly 15 minutes.

To get a bird's-eye perspective of Burgundy, take a microlight flight. Beautiful views of the surrounding vineyards, towns, and countryside will be yours as you soar through the skies in a microlight aircraft. An average microlight flight lasts for roughly 30 minutes.

12. Events and Festivals

12.1 Grapes Harvest Festivals

Known as "Les Vendanges" in French, grape harvest festivals are among the most cherished and important occasions in Burgundy. The climax of the annual grape harvest is celebrated at these festivals, which provide both locals and visitors with a distinctive and immersive experience.

These events usually take place in September, in the late summer or early autumn, when the vineyards are bustling with activity. Because they are based on the grapes' ripening, the precise dates can change from year to year. In Burgundy, harvest festivals are observed in a variety of cities and villages, with each community bringing its own special flair to the celebrations.

The center of these events frequently occurs in the vineyards, where guests can participate in the grape-picking procedure and gain firsthand knowledge of the region's winemaking customs. In Burgundy, grapes are manually harvested to preserve their quality, and visitors are frequently treated to authentic cuisine and wine samples while strolling through the picturesque vineyards.

The "Fête des Vendanges" in Beaune is one of Burgundy's most well-known celebrations of the grape harvest. Wine lovers and tourists from all over the world attend this event to take part in the festivities. Parades, concerts, and fireworks are often part of the festival, which animates the historic town and gives it life.

In addition to Beaune, numerous other Burgundian towns and villages also hold their own special grape harvest celebrations. These celebrations, from Chablis to Nuits-Saint-Georges, offer a close connection to Burgundy's culture, traditions, and people.

Grape harvest celebrations are more than simply a way to appreciate the harvest from the vineyard; they are also a way for the area to demonstrate its dedication to producing top-notch wine. Through these activities, tourists may experience Burgundy's distinct charm while also savoring the harvest's bounty.

12.2 Festivals of Music and Art

Along with having a thriving wine industry, Burgundy also organizes a variety of music and art events that add another layer of cultural richness. These events, which are dispersed over the area, give both established and up-and-coming artists a stage on which to display their abilities. Burgundy's dedication to fostering innovation and cultural variety is reflected in its music and art events.

The Festival Musique et Vin au Clos Vougeot is one of Burgundy's most renowned music events. This magical event takes place in the storied Clos de Vougeot vineyard and combines classical music with Burgundy's best wines. Internationally renowned musicians perform on stage under the open sky, captivating audiences. An extraordinary sensory experience is created when the elegance of the music and the beauty of the vineyard are combined.

The "Festival d'Art Lyrique" in Aix-en-Othe is a true jewel for art lovers. This celebration of opera and lyric art features spellbinding performances in lovely old places. It's a chance to experience the operatic world while taking in Burgundy's picturesque countryside.

For fans of organ music, the "Festival International d'Orgue" in Beaune is delightful. World-class organists perform at old churches and cathedrals throughout the area as part of this festival, filling these architectural wonders with hypnotic sounds.

Dijon's "Nuits d'Orient" event offers a singular blend of Eastern music, art, and culture. This diverse festival, which includes performances, exhibitions, and gastronomic experiences, highlights the rich cultural fabric of the Orient.

Burgundy also holds several art exhibitions throughout the year, such as the "Salon d'Automne" in Auxerre, which presents a wide variety of modern art, and the "Salon des Antiquaires" in Dijon, where collectors of antiquities can peruse a wealth of historical items.

Burgundy's commitment to encouraging cultural diversity and promoting the arts is demonstrated by the music and art festivals that take place there. They are a must-see for culture and art enthusiasts because they provide a singular opportunity to witness the fusion of art, music, and wine against the breathtaking backdrop of this lovely region.

12.3 Wine Festival and Harvest Event

Wine festivals and harvest celebrations in Burgundy are more than just occasions; they pay jubilant respect to the area's long history of winemaking. These events honor the age-old customs that have made Burgundy's wines famous throughout the world and provide a special chance for tourists to become immersed in the region's thriving wine culture.

The "Hospices de Beaune Wine Auction," which takes place on the third Sunday in November, is one of Burgundy's most well-known wine festivals. A prominent event is hosted in the stunning Hospices de Beaune, a prime example of Burgundian construction. The 19th-century auction features remarkable wine lots that regional wineries have given. The combination of history, culture, and philanthropy make it an important event for more than just wine enthusiasts.

A major wine event is the "Fête des Grands Crus" in Chablis. Some of the best Chablis wines, many of which are categorized as Grand Cru, are tasted there. Visitors can speak with winemakers, see the vineyards, and take part in festive events that highlight the region's various terroirs.

The "Fête du Vin" in Nuits-Saint-Georges is a jovial and vibrant occasion where the streets come alive with wine-themed decorations and activities. Visitors can sample a variety of wines from nearby wineries while taking in live entertainment and traditional Burgundian food at this event. The conviviality of Burgundy's wine culture is embodied in this dynamic encounter.

Many communities in Burgundy celebrate the harvest season with smaller-scale celebrations. Parades, regional folk music, and of course, wine tastings serve to commemorate these occasions. Visitors can learn about the precise procedure of gathering the ripe grapes that will soon become superb Burgundy wines by taking part in grape harvesting, or "vendanges," which is a unique and hands-on experience.

Burgundy's wine festivals and harvest festivities pay homage to the region's producers' enthusiasm and commitment. They highlight the interdependence between the locals, the land, and the wines they make. It is possible to experience the vibrant essence of Burgundy's wine culture, taste world-class wines, and make lifelong memories by going to these events.

12.4 Historical Reenactments and customary celebrations

Visitors are transported back in time to discover the rich legacy, customs, and historical moments of Burgundy through historical reenactments and traditional activities. These occasions offer the chance to see Burgundy's past come to life and deepen understanding of its cultural foundations.

A striking historical reenactment occasion is the "Fêtes de la Vigne" in Montmartin-en-Graignes. It honors the famous 12th-century trip to the area by King Henry II and his wife, Eleanor of Aquitaine. The entire community is transformed into a medieval scene, complete with costumed actors, jousting contests, and traditional craftspeople showcasing their abilities. The celebration serves as a stark reminder of Burgundy's historical importance and its ties to the European royal courts.

Another fascinating event that transports tourists back in time is "Les Médiévales de Semur-en-Auxois". Knights, minstrels, and craftspeople who recreate the atmosphere of medieval life take the stage in the town of Semur-en-Auxois because of its beautifully preserved medieval architecture. Visitors are transported to a bygone era by jousting, troubadours, and people dressed in period attire, demonstrating Burgundy's historical accuracy.

Digoin's "Fête de l'Escargot" is a peculiar but lovable celebration that honors Burgundy's gastronomic heritage. This festival honors escargot, a specialty of French cuisine. Visitors can sample escargot prepared in various ways and discover the conventional techniques for rearing snails. It's an opportunity to embrace regional cuisine and acquaint oneself with its culinary traditions.

The "Fête des Sarments" in Santenay is a delightful event that recreates the old traditions of vineyard management for individuals who are interested in Burgundy's viticultural past. Participants provide insight into the historical craftsmanship that molded Burgundy's winemaking legacy by demonstrating how vines were pruned and managed in the past.

Burgundy's historical reenactments and customary celebrations offer a fascinating voyage through time. Any visit to this culturally rich region of France would benefit from them as they give a deeper grasp of the area's history, culture, and culinary delights.

13. Perfect 7-14 Days Itinerary

13.1 Day by Day 7-Days Itinerary with Highlights

Burgundy may be well balanced in terms of its historical, culinary, and natural treasures by being explored in seven days. This itinerary's day-by-day breakdown blends well-known sights with undiscovered gems to make for an amazing trip:

Arrival in Dijon on Day 1:
- Arrive in Dijon, the Burgundy region's capital, and settle into your lodging.
- Take a tour of the historic center to see the well-preserved medieval and Renaissance buildings.
- The exquisite tombs of the Palace of the Dukes of Burgundy (Palais des Ducs) are not to be missed.
- A traditional Burgundian dinner at a nearby restaurant.

Day Two of the Dijon Exploration:

Spend the morning visiting the thriving food market Les Halles de Dijon and sample some local delicacies.

- View the stunning art collection at the Musée des Beaux-Arts.
- Drive to Beaune in the afternoon, the center of the Côte d'Or wine region.
- Stroll through the quaint streets of Beaune and eat in a neighborhood café.

Day 3: Wine tasting in Beaune:

- Start the day with a trip to the Hospices de Beaune, a revered example of Gothic design.
- At the Marché aux Vins, where you may taste some of the best wines in the area, learn about Burgundy's wine culture.
- Take a leisurely bike ride or drive through the nearby vineyards in the afternoon.
- After dinner, head over to Beaune to sample some regional wines.

The Côte de Nuits Vineyards on Day Four:

- Travel north to the Côte de Nuits, where some of the most renowned vineyards are found.
- Visit Gevrey-Chambertin, Vosne-Romanée, and Nuits-Saint-Georges, three lovely villages.
- Attend wine tasting events at well-known wineries.
- Indulge in a typical Burgundian lunch at a nearby restaurant.

Morvan Natural Park, Day 5:
- Travel to the tranquil Morvan Natural Park, which is noted for its forests and lakes.
- Enjoy the pristine waters by renting a boat or hiking along gorgeous trails.
- Travel to Vézelay, a quaint village with the UNESCO-listed Basilica of Sainte-Marie-Madeleine.
- Go back to the park's lodging of your choice for a peaceful evening.

<u>Chablis and Vézelay on Day 6:</u>
- Take a tour of the Chablis area, which is known for its crisp white wines.

- Explore the city's historic district and sample some local wine.
- Continue on to Vézelay to explore its charming streets and take in its elegant atmosphere.
- For a tranquil evening, spend the night at Vézelay or a nearby town.

Day 7: Arrival in Auxerre and departure

- Spend your final morning at Vézelay or take a leisurely stroll in the park.
- Visit the city of Auxerre, which is renowned for its magnificent cathedral and quaint old town.
- Explore the riverfront while taking in one last Burgundian lunch.
- Depart from the closest airport, train station, or Auxerre.

A well-rounded experience of Burgundy is provided by this 7-day tour, which combines historical landmarks, wine exploration, scenic beauty, and culinary delights. However, Burgundy has a lot more to offer, so you might decide to stay longer to find more undiscovered gems.

13.2 Recommendations that Are Off the Beaten Path

While Burgundy's well-known tourist attractions are alluring, there are hidden jewels that provide distinctive and enlightening encounters. For those seeking less-traveled routes in Burgundy, here are some suggestions:

1. Cluny: Take a tour of this historic town, which was formerly the site of the renowned Cluny Abbey, a major hub of medieval European culture. The ruins of the abbey offer evidence of its previous splendor, and nearby lies the National Stud Farm, which is devoted to maintaining French horse breeds.

2. Brancion: This hilltop settlement from the Middle Ages is a well-kept secret. There is a timeless quality to its old streets and old structures. Insight into Burgundy's feudal past is provided by the Château de Brancion, and the village's expansive views are spectacular.

**3. Visit the magnificent Renaissance Château d'Ancy-le-Franc, a lesser-known jewel of Burgundy, in Ancy-le-Franc. Its outstanding interior design and amazing architecture are authentic representations of the Renaissance period.

**4. Flavigny-sur-Ozerain: **A charming village with well-preserved medieval alleyways and rich history, Flavigny-sur-Ozerain is well-known for its anise candy. The absence of crowds makes it a tranquil location to explore.

5. Fontenay Abbey: Fontenay Abbey is a UNESCO World Heritage property that is tucked away in a serene valley. The beautiful Romanesque building and well-preserved Cistercian abbey provide an insight into monastic life.

**6. Families and environment lovers will love the Parc de l'Auxois, a wildlife park close to Semur-en-Auxois. It offers opportunities for up-close experiences with the indigenous flora and is home to a variety of wildlife, including European bison.

13.3 Ideas to Make the Most of Your Time

Take into account these suggestions to make the most of your seven-day trip to Burgundy and make it seamless and memorable:

**1. Plan ahead: To make the most of your time, do your research and create a detailed itinerary in advance. Decide which sites and activities are most important to you.

**2. Making reservations in advance for tours and wine tastings at well-known wineries is a good idea, particularly during busy times of the year.

**3. **Pack judiciously and just bring what you really need to ensure a comfortable and quick trip.

**4. Local cuisine is an essential component of the Burgundian experience; try local foods and wines wherever you go.

5. Time management: Utilize your transfer time by taking in the lovely villages and scenery you pass through.

**6. Local Advice: **Ask locals for advice or insider knowledge without hesitation. They frequently are aware of the best-kept secrets.

7. Explore on Foot: It is preferable to explore Burgundy's many cities and villages on foot, so wear suitable walking shoes.

**8. Enjoy the Moment: **Slow down and take your time to appreciate Burgundy's beauty, flavors, and culture. It's a place where a leisurely pace of life is best appreciated.

You may make the most of your seven-day vacation in Burgundy and make priceless memories that will last a lifetime with a well-planned itinerary, an openness to learning, and respect for the local traditions.

14. Practical Advice and Suggestions

14.1 Information on Health and Safety

Like the majority of France, Burgundy is a safe region to visit, but for a hassle-free and enjoyable trip, it's important to be aware of general safety and health advice.

Safety:

Burgundy is renowned for its security and lack of crime. But you should still exercise common sense care. Be cautious with your possessions, especially in crowded places, and keep valuables hidden. Additionally, it's a good idea to make copies of critical documents in case they are lost or stolen.

Health:

1. Medical Care: Burgundy provides top-notch medical care. Holders of a European Health Insurance Card

(EHIC) have access to public healthcare. Visitors from outside the EU should have complete travel insurance.

2. vaccines: Regular vaccines must be current. Consult your doctor for the appropriate immunizations based on your trip itinerary and medical background.

3. Food and Drink: Burgundy is renowned for its delectable cuisine. Although the tap water in your area is mostly safe to drink, bottled water is widely accessible if you have any doubts. As with any travel destination, observe sanitary food handling procedures while savoring the local cuisine.

4. Pharmacies: Pharmacies (pharmacies in French) are widely available and helpful for minor health issues. Although the staff there frequently speaks English, it still helps to be familiar with generic drug names.

5. When traveling in the summer, remember to pack sunscreen, sunglasses, and a hat. Especially while

visiting vineyards and other outdoor locations, the sun can be very powerful.

Emergency contact numbers:
For general emergencies, phone 112, and for medical assistance, dial 15.

14.2 Language and Regional Protocol

Language:
Burgundy's official language is French. Although many people working in the tourism sector speak English, particularly in well-known locations, it is courteous to be familiar with a few basic French expressions. Your efforts to communicate with the locals in their language are appreciated. Here are several necessities:

- "Bonjour" (bohn-zhoor) - Salutation of the day
- Thank you. "Merci" (mehr-see)
- "S'il vous plaît" (seel voo pleh) means "Thank you"
- Yes, "Oui" (wee).

- "Non" (noh) means "not"

Local Protocol

1. In France, it's usual to welcome friends by kissing them on both cheeks. In more formal contexts, handshakes are expected.

2. When visiting cathedrals, churches, or premium eateries, please dress neatly. For most other places, casual clothing is acceptable.

3. Service charge is included in restaurant invoices, but tipping is customarily done with spare change. It's customary to reward hotel personnel for exceptional service by rounding up cab fees.

4. Punctuality: Arrive on time for all scheduled events. It's a token of deference.

5. Keep your wrists up while seated at the table, and remember to say "Bon appétit" before beginning your

meal. Finishing everything on your plate is considered courteous.

Cultural sensitivity:

- Dress modestly and cover your knees and shoulders while entering any place of worship, including churches and cathedrals.

- Show respect for regional traditions and customs, especially in smaller towns and villages.

14.3 Currency and Financial Issues

Currency:

The Euro (€) is the official currency of Burgundy and all of France. While coins come in cents and euros, banknotes come in a variety of denominations. For cash withdrawals, ATMs are extensively available in towns and cities. The majority of facilities, including restaurants, hotels, and shops, accept major credit and debit cards.

Financial Concerns:

1. Currency Exchange: Airports, banks, and exchange offices all offer currency exchange services. For little purchases, it is wise to carry some cash in euros.

2. Credit Cards: Visa, MasterCard, and, to a lesser extent, American Express, are the three most widely accepted credit cards. To prevent card problems, let your bank know about your vacation intentions.

3. Service charge is included in restaurant invoices, but tipping is customarily done with spare change. Tipping hotel personnel for outstanding service is often considered polite.

4. Shopping: Credit cards are accepted at most large retailers. Smaller businesses, meanwhile, could favor cash. Local merchants and street marketplaces frequently only accept cash.

5. ATMs are widely accessible in towns and cities. When exploring remote areas, be sure to have enough cash on

hand because certain rural areas may not be easily accessible.

6. Bills and Receipts: Save your receipts in case you qualify for the "tax-free shopping" program, which could result in tax returns on purchases. Make sure to ask about it at the participating retailers.

14.4 Communication and the Internet

Burgundy has a well-established infrastructure for internet and communication services, making it simple to stay connected. What you need to know is as follows:

1. Internet Accessibility
- Wi-Fi: In urban areas, the majority of hotels, eateries, cafes, and tourist destinations offer free Wi-Fi to patrons. Signs showing the presence of Wi-Fi hotspots are frequently seen.

- **Data Roaming:** You can utilize mobile data to stay connected if you have a global data plan. For information on coverage and roaming costs, contact your cellphone provider.

2. Mobile phone services include:
- The mobile network in France is strong and offers good coverage, especially in remote locations.

- Important carriers include Bouygues Telecom, SFR, and Orange. These suppliers sell prepaid SIM cards for your phone, which you can buy from them at local shops or airports.

- The universal emergency number in the European Union is 112, which can be used to contact emergency services.

3. Postal Services
- La Poste, the French postal service, operates effectively and consistently. Local post offices allow you to ship packages and mail.

- Post offices typically are open during the week, with shortened hours on Saturdays, and are frequently closed on Sundays.

4. Communication Advice:
- Although many people working in the Burgundy tourism business understand English, knowing a few basic French phrases will come in handy and be appreciated by locals.

- The 24-hour clock is frequently used in France, so become accustomed to using it for timetables and appointments.
- Be sure to allow extra time for overseas delivery when sending postcards or letters.

14.5 Highlights of Local Customs and Culture

Not only is Burgundy a location of great beauty and wine, but it's also a place where deeply ingrained traditions and cultural landmarks have a big impact on daily life:

1. Wine Culture: Burgundy's identity is rooted in its wine culture. A cultural highlight is taking part in wine tastings and vineyard tours. Don't forget to swirl your glass, take in the smells of the wine, and chat with the producers.

2. Festivals and customs: You may fully experience Burgundy's customs by taking part in regional events like grape harvest festivals and historical reenactments. One of the most prestigious occasions, the Hospices de Beaune Wine Auction draws wine connoisseurs from all over the world.

3. Burgundy's food is well-known throughout the world. Classic dishes like Coq au Vin (chicken in wine sauce) and Boeuf Bourguignon (beef stew) shouldn't be missed. To get the real deal, serve these with local wines.

4. With architectural marvels like the Basilica of Sainte-Marie-Madeleine in Vézelay and the ancient town of Autun, the area is rich in art and history. Discover these locations to appreciate Burgundy's aesthetic and historical features.

5. Respect regional customs, such as the French greeting of kissing both cheeks when welcoming friends. In French culture, courtesy and politeness are highly regarded.

6. Visit a market: The markets in Burgundy are lively and genuine. Discover fresh fruit, cheeses, and handcrafted goods in your neighborhood markets. Price fixing is the norm; haggling is uncommon.

7. When visiting churches and cathedrals, dress appropriately by covering your knees and shoulders with modest apparel. When dining in fancy establishments, be well-groomed.

8. Wine & cuisine Pairing: Learn the art of combining wine and cuisine. Local eateries frequently offer suggestions for matching particular wines with dishes, improving your eating experience.

9. Enjoy the Slow Pace: Burgundy represents a leisurely way of life. Spend some time enjoying the moment, discovering charming villages, and relaxing in the serene settings of the area.

14.6 Services and Emergency Contacts

It's crucial to be familiar with the local emergency numbers and services in case of an emergency while visiting Burgundy:

1. Medical emergencies
- Dial 15 for medical assistance. You will be connected with the relevant medical services by the operator.

2. Police-Related and Other Emergencies:

- Dial 112 in the event of a general emergency. You can reach a variety of emergency services, such as the police and medical aid, by dialing this number.

3. Department of Fire:
- In the event of a fire emergency, dial 18. Quick aid will be given by the fire department.

4. Consulate and Embassy Information:
- Make sure you have the address and phone number of the embassy or consulate of your country in case you need assistance. In bigger cities like Paris, you can find a variety of embassies and consulates.

5. Travel protection:
- Make sure you have adequate travel insurance before you leave so that it will cover unforeseen circumstances like medical emergencies and trip cancellations. Keep the details of your insurance in plain sight.

6. Pharmacies:

- Pharmacies, or pharmacies in French, are widely distributed and can be used for non-emergency medical issues. They frequently have English-speaking employees and can offer advice on simple medical problems.

When visiting Burgundy, it's critical to have a thorough awareness of emergency procedures and contact information to ensure you can promptly and effectively obtain assistance if necessary.

Made in United States
North Haven, CT
30 September 2024